FLORIDA

AND THE BAHAMAS

Martin Gostelow

JPMGUIDES

Contents

Fold-out map

Florida

Miami

Orlando

This Way Florida

The peninsula of Florida (bigger than England) juts out from Georgia nearly all the way to Cuba. In the north, the Panhandle, stretching out towards Alabama and Louisiana, maintains close ties with the Deep South, while the Keys flirt with Caribbean personality and atmosphere. Its contrasts will take you aback. The renovated Art Deco façades of Miami painted in ice-cream colours, the golden beaches, palm trees and countless theme parks, each one more audacious than the last, leave you with a veritable kaleidoscope of impressions whirling around in your mind.

Florida is home to spacemen and sports stars, millionaires and pensioners. Not to mention alligators, acrobatic dolphins and Mickey Mouse. With every sort of water sport, unlimited tennis and golf, lake and sea fishing, inland adventures and a surprising measure of culture, there's more to see and do here than anyone has time for.

The climate is subtropical: every winter Floridians and visitors smugly read about snowstorms wreaking havoc in the north, while Miami basks in the nation's highest temperatures. Listening to people talking, you'll hear some soft southern drawls, but so many immigrants have brought their own accents from Cuba, Haiti or New York that the state is more multi-cultural than most. Allowed to settle in the US under a special law, the Cubans introduced their music, the game called *jai alai*, strong coffee and the Spanish language. In fact, in Miami you could probably go for a whole day without hearing English spoken.

A Little Geography

Florida is flat, its highest point a mere 105 m (345 ft) above sea level. The coastline, much of it bordered by beaches of white or golden sand, stretches 2,200 km (1,370 miles)—far more if you count all the offshore islands. Seas are generally calmer and warmer on the Gulf of Mexico than the Atlantic side of the peninsula.

Inland, millions of cattle graze the grassy plains, and great tracts of land are planted with groves of orange and grapefruit trees—Florida is the biggest citrus-growing region in the world.

From the 1,800 sq km (700 sq miles) of Lake Okeechobee ("big water" in Seminole) and an estimated 30,000 smaller lakes, warm water seeps through the unique wetlands of the Everglades, culminating in mangrove swamps at the tip of the state. No doubt it seemed a good idea at the time when, in 1905, Governor Napoleon Bonaparte Broward lifted the first shovelful of earth, beginning the digging of countless canals designed to drain swampland and turn it over to farming and building. Now an awareness of the area's delicate ecology has led to a remarkable change of thinking. In 1989, President Bush signed a bill directing the US Army's engineers to restore a more natural flow of water into the Everglades.

From the mainland, the world's longest overseas causeway links a chain of islands known as the Florida Keys. The coral reefs that shield them, fatal to many ships in the past, now attract hosts of scuba-divers and snorkellers. The road ends at Key West, where a famously laidback lifestyle has drawn all sorts of escapists and eccentrics: some who came for a visit stayed for ever.

The Good Life

Newcomers are invariably impressed by the facilities they find in Florida. You can eat well on a modest budget, and accommodation offers value for money. The best way to get around is by car. Orlando and its theme parks and indeed all of Florida are practically designed around the automobile. In the smaller towns, parking problems have yet to reach crisis levels. And for out-of-town excursions the car permits spur-of-the-moment decisions and detours that often provide the unexpected pleasures which turn out to be the most memorable of your trip.

HURRICANE!

The definition, a wind above 120 kph (75 mph), tells only half the story. Wind speeds can reach twice that figure, accompanied by torrential rain and huge waves. The hurricane season lasts from June to November, and in a typical year one of them will hit the coast somewhere in the southeastern US. But your chance of experiencing one of these mighty storms is slight indeed. They're a lot more predictable these days. Advanced tracking systems give plenty of warning, time enough to batten down the hatches and evacuate people from exposed areas. Radar, hurricane-hunter flights, satellite pictures and forecasts combine to produce a formal "hurricane watch", which goes into effect 24 hours before a major storm is expected.

Flashback

First Floridians

Small groups of hunters and gatherers moved in to northern Florida about 18,000 years ago, migrating from further north and west. Later spreading down the peninsula, they lived on the plentiful game and especially the abundant shellfish. Near swampy inlets along the southern coast, mounds of empty oyster shells piled up by these early inhabitants are still the only "hills" to be seen in the flat landscape.

As numbers grew, so did tribal structures: there is evidence of organized religion in the ceremonial burial sites dating from around 2000 BC. The next stage was the growing of crops—corn (maize), squash and peppers, for example—sometimes on former swampland which had been drained by quite elaborate systems of ditches. At the time that European explorers appeared on the scene, the land which now forms Florida was divided among five distinct Native American ("Indian") nations, totalling perhaps 100,000 people.

The Europeans Arrive

Columbus never reached the American mainland, but one of his companions, the Spaniard Juan Ponce de León explored the Florida coast in 1513. He failed to find the fabled Fountain of Youth, or the hoped-for gold, but reported to the King of Spain that the peninsula was promising territory for settlement. In 1521, he led a party of would-be colonists to Charlotte Harbour on the west coast, but they were attacked by hostile Calusa Indians. Ponce de León was killed, and his followers retreated to Cuba.

Further attempts at establishing a permanent presence also ended in disaster, until, to neutralize a threat from France, Pedro Menéndez founded a fortified colony in 1565 at St Augustine, today proclaimed to be the oldest city in the United States. It was sacked and burned in 1586 by the English buccaneer Sir Francis Drake, but was rebuilt with more powerful defences.

Rival Empires

French explorers had claimed the Mississippi valley for France, right down to the mouth of the great river where they were to found the port of New Orleans. Pressing down from their colonies to the north, the British invaded Florida during the War of the Spanish Succession (1701–

14) and wiped out most of Spain's handful of settlements. Then in 1763, Spain gave up its remaining enclaves on the Florida coast in exchange for the return of its key Caribbean port, Havana in Cuba, which Britain had captured a year earlier.

When the Spanish moved out of the mainland, British settlers from Alabama and Georgia took over. With them came a collection of American Indians called Seminoles (from *cimarrones*, Spanish for "runaway" or "wild"), displacing the original inhabitants who were forced westward or accompanied the Spanish to Cuba.

Joining the USA
During the American Revolution, Florida remained loyal to the British crown, but when Britain conceded defeat in 1783, it handed Florida back to Spain. American settlers flooded in, and Spain, unable to control them, was forced to sell Florida to the United States in 1819.

General Andrew Jackson, victorious against the British at the end of the War of 1812, became the territory's first governor. From then on, the settlers were able to call on the help of the US Army to force the Seminoles off the best land and into the swamps.

In 1830, Jackson, now US president, signed a draconian law requiring all American Indians to leave the eastern states, including Florida. Some complied, taking the "trail of tears" to reservations in the west. Others refused and retreated further into the depths of the Everglades, emerging to engage the army in hit-and-run warfare. Their leader Osceola was seized when negotiating under a flag of truce and died in prison. The war ended in stalemate in 1842. The few hundred remaining Indians were left in their remote settlements, where today their descendants run tourist attractions.

Civil War and Recovery
In 1845, Florida became the 27th state of the Union. Political power was mainly in the hands of plantation owners who relied on slave labour, so Florida backed the South and joined the Confederacy in the Civil War. However, Union forces soon captured the main ports and from then on Florida was aloof from the fighting. When the war ended in 1865, the slaves were nominally free, although many carried on working for their former owners and their lives didn't change very much.

The destruction caused by the war was less in Florida than elsewhere in the South, and recovery was quicker, driven by northern investors. In the forefront were two railroad magnates: Henry Flagler who pushed his tracks down the east coast; and Henry Plant, who built the Gulf Coast line to Tampa and beyond. There had already been a few pioneer vacationers, escaping northern winters; now the way was open for tourism—and settlement— on a grander scale. Flagler and Plant put up luxury hotels to house the new visitors in style. Freight trains carried Florida's citrus fruit and prime beef to the markets of the north.

Property prices soared in the 1920s as buyers poured into the state, intent on buying a place in the sun. Then came news of swindles and bank failures. A devastating hurricane killed more than 100 in Miami, shattering confidence as well as houses. The real estate market collapsed and many were left with worthless pieces of paper, or the title to an undrained piece of alligator-infested swamp.

When Wall Street crashed in 1929, followed by the Great Depression, the party was over, at least for the time being. A cautious revival began in the 1930s, when the Art Deco hotels were built in Miami Beach, but it would be quite a while before the good times would start to roll again.

World War II and After

Millions of recruits to the US armed forces were sent to Florida for training, and thousands of new migrants were attracted by defence-related jobs. Those who had never before left their homes in the industrial cities of the north were captivated by the clean, green spaces, the warm blue seas and mild winters. Many resolved to return after the war, either for vacations or to settle, raise families and retire.

In 1947 Cape Canaveral was selected as the site of a missile test base. Momentum picked up after the Soviet Union launched *Sputnik*, the first earth satellite, and then put Yuri Gagarin in orbit. Shocked, the United States responded with a massive expansion of its own space programme and the first batch of trainee US astronauts arrived. Even before John Glenn's first orbital flight in 1962, President Kennedy had announced the objective of putting an American on the moon before the end of the decade. That entailed huge expenditure and an influx of highly paid engineers, and the area prospered. The 1960s were years of glory at the Cape. Crowds of a million and more used to gather to watch the huge rockets blast off, and the series of Apollo missions was climaxed by the promised lunar landing in 1969. Nowadays, Space Shuttle launches are almost routine, but they're still a thrilling sight and there's the bonus of seeing the shuttles return, gliding in to land on the Kennedy Space Center's runway.

The Jet Age

Walt Disney World, inaugurated in 1971, soon became the world's most visited tourist attraction. It transformed the economy of cen-

THE INTRA-COASTAL WATERWAY

Small craft, and some not so small, can make their way along most of the coast of Florida and up the US eastern seaboard without needing to risk the rigours of the open sea. Islands had always offered a protected passage between themselves and the mainland, but during World War II, lagoons and even rivers parallel to the coast were dredged and linked up to create thousands of kilometres of sheltered channels. It wasn't just for the comfort of pleasure sailors: the waterway's planners were also concerned to keep commercial shipping away from the threat of enemy submarines. An ambitious scheme to cut a deepwater canal right across Florida was never carried out.

tral Florida, creating—directly and indirectly—as many as 100,000 jobs and 80,000 hotel rooms. In just a few years Orlando turned from a sleepy backwater concerned primarily with the markets for oranges and cattle into a gleaming boom city with a busy international airport. (Now it has two.)

Big jets, low fares and package deals allowed millions of Europeans to join the tens of millions of Americans and Canadians who regularly spend their holidays toasting under the Florida sun. Miami gave its Art Deco district a new lick of paint; and it suddenly lost its reputation as a retirement home. People discovered the Gulf Coast too, and to the delight of hoteliers all over the state, extended the season from winter to most of the year.

CUBAN CONNECTION

Cuba, the giant among the Caribbean islands, lies only 180 km (112 miles) south of Key West, the nearest US territory. After 400 years of Spanish rule, it became a republic in 1898. But independence was limited: it was an economic colony of the United States, presided over by a succession of corrupt dictators.

In 1959, after a two-year guerrilla campaign, Fidel Castro and fewer than a thousand supporters overthrew the old regime, took power and launched a socialist revolution. US-owned property was seized and private businesses nationalized, and 300,000 Cubans, mostly from the middle classes, fled to Miami. The US government broke off relations and in 1961 launched the disastrous Bay of Pigs invasion by some of the émigrés. Castro formed ever-closer ties with the Soviet Union.

As life became more difficult in Cuba there were campaigns in the US for easier emigration. In 1980, Castro craftily responded by emptying his jails and mental hospitals and sending to the US the illiterate and unemployable, a total of 120,000 he was happy to be rid of.

When the Soviet Union collapsed, Cuba was left friendless, its economy in dire straits. People risked their lives by putting to sea on homemade rafts, or by taking refuge in the US base at Guantanamo Bay on Cuba, as a stepping stone to Florida. Miami's million Cubans, overwhelmingly anti-Castro, form a powerful lobby against any post-Cold War moves to talk to Cuba. No politician can ignore them.

On the Scene

To thousands of holiday-makers, Florida is synonymous with Miami and its sister across the bay, the resort of Miami Beach. It's here that you'll find the extravagant tastes that have become an intrinsic part of the American legend. In this land, people have waved magic wands to create the most elaborate fantasies: Disney World, Cape Canaveral, Vizcaya, Miami itself are all realizations of dreams. When the glitter gets too much, head for the wilderness of the Everglades, go fishing on the Keys, or soak up some culture along the Gulf Coast.

▶ MIAMI
Downtown, Miami Beach, Key Biscayne, Coconut Grove, Coral Gables, Southern Outskirts

The city, now so vast and vibrant, began as a small US Army fort in the Seminole Wars of the 1830s. Later, speculators bought slices of land for $1 each, and the government offered tracts of territory free to adventurous spirits who could defend them against all-comers for five years. But even as late as 1870 the population of Dade County, including Miami, numbered a mere 85.

By 1896, it had grown to 343. The place was declared to be a city, the street plan was marked out, and Henry Flagler's railroad arrived. He had been enticed to build it this far by a rich widow, Julia Tuttle, whose dream was to bring prosperity to south Florida. When a hard winter destroyed Flagler's citrus crops further north, she sent him orange blossom from Miami to prove it was frost-free.

Today the city is like a Latin American metropolis. Out of a population of more than 3.5 million, over half are Spanish-speaking, the great majority of them Cuban immigrants and their descendants. There's a large Haitian colony, too, and in other enclaves the shop signs are in Russian, Greek, Italian and Vietnamese. The black community has grown

in numbers but declined as a percentage (to around 20 per cent) as a result of the Hispanic influx. Racial tensions between the various groups have sometimes exploded into violence, and traffic in illegal drugs remains a major problem for the authorities.

Downtown

After years of decline, the city centre has been spectacularly reborn, with the gleaming glass towers of banks, hotels and public buildings creating a futuristic skyline. The arcaded Metro-Dade Cultural Center at 101 West Flagler Street is big enough to house an auditorium, the Center for the Fine Arts with an art gallery and sculpture court, Miami's public library and the Historical Museum of Southern Florida.

The automated Metromover makes an elevated loop around the downtown area; it's more for fun than actually getting anywhere. Serious commuters take the Metrorail system to and from the northwestern and southwestern suburbs.

Flagler Street meets Biscayne Boulevard, the north-south avenue near the waterfront, at Bayfront Park, a green space where there's often a concert or other free entertainment. Next to it, the Bayside Marketplace shopping, eating and leisure complex has successfully breathed new life into a formerly rundown area. Here too is the starting point for boat tours of the harbour and bay.

Across a high drawbridge is the Port of Miami and its cruise terminal: who knows, the sight of

DON'T GET LOST!

Miami was laid out as a grid of straight lines and right angles, like most cities in the US, but on a grand scale for a time when the population could still be counted in hundreds. Nowadays, with the suburbs stretching for 50 km (30 miles) and more, including areas where you're advised not to drive—and certainly not to walk—it's as well to know where you are.

Flagler Street, the main east-west axis of downtown Miami, counts as the "zero" for the street numbering scheme. The north-south avenues are numbered from Miami Avenue. These two create four quadrants, NE, SE, SW and NW, which appear in addresses. When driving, make sure that you know where you are going, and that you have a good street map. If at all possible, get directions from a local expert.

great white ships sailing off to the Caribbean might just tempt you to change your holiday plans.

Little Havana

The Cuban community has never stopped growing, and the sector of the city that it dominates is no longer so little. Beginning downtown, it spreads west along a 30-block stretch of SW 8th Street, literally translated as *Calle Ocho*, and into the streets and avenues north and south. Restaurants specialize in Cuban, Mexican and other Latin American cuisine, and streetside snack bars serve little cups of strong and aromatic *café cubano*. By night, *discotecas* pulsate to the latest Latin sounds.

Little Haiti

Perennial troubles in their Caribbean homeland, the poorest nation in the Americas, brought waves of Haitians to the US in hope of something better. Many of Miami's 200,000 Haitians live around 1st and 2nd Avenues NE, north of the Julia Tuttle Causeway to Miami Beach. People here speak Creole, derived from French and various African languages; shops and cafés are gaudily painted, markets sell tropical produce and Haitian food.

Miami Beach

At the beginning of the 20th century the long, narrow island across North Biscayne Bay was nothing but mangrove swamp infested by snakes and mosquitoes. It took infinite determination and thousands of tonnes of white sand to turn it into America's best-known beach resort, lined with a wall of hotels and apartments. Causeways, up to 5 km (3 miles) long, link it to the mainland north of the city centre.

Sometime in the 1950s, the rich and famous stopped coming. Miami Beach dropped out of fashion and a few years ago was in the doldrums, shabby and dowdy. Then, suddenly, the old resort was "in" again. The Art Deco District of South Beach, from 5th to around 21st Street, underwent a dramatic rebirth. Nowhere else in the United States are there so many buildings (800 of them!) from the jazz age, bright with chrome, streamlined ceramics, coloured glass and Aztec motifs. Now most of them have been restored and repainted in the original pastel shades of the 1930s and 40s. Some of the best are along Ocean Drive, between 5th and 15th Streets, where small hotels and restaurants face the sea across a green expanse of grass. From dusk until the small hours, this is *the* place to see and be seen, as it is often alive with film crews, models and movie stars exploiting the classy backdrop and vibrant nightlife.

15

Miami's Art Deco district is an appetizing display of ice-cream colours.

Displays in the Bass Museum of Art (on Park Avenue near 21st Street) tell the story of the local architecture in models, photos and drawings. And its varied collections of paintings from every era of western art are a credit to the philanthropic Miami Beach residents who donated most of them.

The beach itself is a broad and flat expanse of sand, bordered from 21st Street to 46th Street by a "boardwalk", a wooden promenade punctuated by covered pavilions and seats. Between the beach and Collins Avenue, the main artery of the island, the vast Fontainebleau Hilton (here they say "Fount'n-blue") is a lot more than a hotel. This symbol of Miami Beach in its 1950s heyday still lives on—modernized, redecorated and minus much of the kitsch.

At the top end of Miami Beach are the glitzy shops of Bal Harbour (they use the English spelling). A bridge carries the road (the coast-hugging A1A) to the Sunny Isles, a relaxed beach and fishing resort. Close by on the mainland is the "oldest building in North America", the cloisters of St Bernard brought stone by stone from Spain by William Randolph Hearst and rebuilt here in the 1950s.

Key Biscayne

The graceful arc of Rickenbacker Causeway soars over Biscayne Bay for 5 km (3 miles) to an offshore island known for its desirable residences. Halfway along, on Virginia Key, is the Seaquarium, where leaping dolphins and a killer whale do their stunts. At the end of the causeway is a popular public beach park and a tennis stadium where the world's best have played.

The southern end of the island, past those expensive houses, is a State Recreation Area where local people like to picnic under the trees that line the beach. The restored 1825 Cape Florida lighthouse is open for visits. Climb to the top of its 30-m (98-ft) tower for a great view across the bay, back to the city, or out to some ramshackle old fishing platforms which have somehow survived several hurricanes.

Coconut Grove

An easy-going community of artists and professionals on the shores of the bay, "The Grove" is a delightful mixture of open-air cafés and restaurants, stylish boutiques and bohemian life. Sunset is the signal for a party, and music begins to blare from bars and cars while roller bladers slice through the traffic.

City Hall

Down at the yacht harbour, filled with pleasure craft, notice the little white Art Deco building now serving as the City Hall. It used to be the passenger terminal for Pan American Airways flying boats taking off for Cuba and South America in the 1930s. You can still see the airline's "winged globe" logo on the façade.

The Barnacle

This old wooden house dates from the early years of Coconut Grove in the late 19th century, before Miami existed. It was built for Commodore Ralph Munroe from the timber of ships wrecked off this coast, notoriously dangerous in the days before modern navigational aids. Munroe was one of the first photographers in south Florida, and the pictures on display are a unique archive.

1 **THE BEST BEACH** An island joined by a causeway to the Gulf coast near Sarasota, **Siesta Key** claims the world's whitest sand, which is soft and fine in texture—just right for building sandcastles. This, plus the broad, gently sloping beach makes it a perfect place to bring children.

Villa Vizcaya

Long before the speculative rush to Florida, the industrialist James Deering of the International Harvester family was looking for somewhere to put his personal harvest of international art. In 1912 he hired a thousand craftsmen to create Villa Vizcaya, a palace in Italian Renaissance style on Biscayne Bay, just south of the Rickenbacker Causeway entrance. You can tour the house and marvel at Deering's eclectic taste: he gathered many of the architectural features from palaces in Italy, monasteries in Spain and castles in Ireland.

Across the highway, the Museum of Science has plenty of hands-on and other interactive exhibits, while its adjacent Planetarium presents various fascinating aspects of astronomy in fast-paced shows.

Coral Gables

Laid out in the 1920s, this wealthy community was one of the earliest examples of a planned garden suburb, full of fountains, tropical greenery and mock-Spanish architecture. Sadly, the developer, George Merrick, went bust when the property market collapsed, but his vision has survived. The area's prosperity today is evident from the quality of shopping and the restaurants, some of Miami's finest.

The Lowe Art Museum, on the campus of the University of Miami, displays a cross-section of everything from native American to 17th-century Spanish paintings, on to modern art.

Southern Outskirts

The Fairchild Tropical Botanic Garden is the biggest and one of the best of its kind in the United States, covering 32 ha (80 acres) with an estimated 7,000 species of plants. During World War II, pilots were brought here to train in jungle survival techniques in case they were shot down in the tropics.

At the neighbouring Parrot Jungle Island, the birds will eat out of your hand, ride bicycles, roller skate and generally fascinate the kids with their amazing antics.

Further south, the big, modern Metrozoo gives the animals space to roam, using clever design to put you surprisingly close to white Bengal tigers, gorillas and many other species in complete safety.

Opposite the main entrance to the Metrozoo, the Gold Coast Railroad Museum has several historic locomotives and rolling stock. You can also see the presidential sleeping cars in which presidents Roosevelt, Truman, Eisenhower, Reagan and Bush have travelled.

THE EVERGLADES

Less than an hour's drive from Miami and its bustle, you can wander alone in a vast sub-tropical wilderness. As flat as a table, it's still a landscape of great variety. Wide open prairies of sawgrass (a sharp-toothed sedge) are interrupted by pockets of woodland; tracts of steaming jungle merge into deep, dark mangrove swamps as you approach the sea. There's no fixed shoreline; thousands of islands are separated by a maze of tidal mud flats and waterways, home and breeding ground for countless birds and fish.

In early times, various Native American tribes lived as hunter-gatherers in this part of the world: in some places you can still see the mounds of oyster shells they discarded. In the 19th century, several hundred Seminole settled here, and their descendants, the Miccosukee, still have a village but depend on the tourist trade for a living.

For the last 150 years, the delicately balanced ecology of the Everglades has been threatened by encroaching urban development, agro-chemicals and ill-considered drainage schemes. Fragile as it may be, the big swamp makes an eye-opening change of scene from the beach. You can watch alligators in their element, even from your car window as they lie beside—or sometimes on—the road. Resident birds include the osprey, the swallow-tailed kite, the bald eagle, herons, egrets, ibis, roseate spoonbills and other stately waders. But be warned that one other winged beast is here in abundance: the mosquito. That's one good reason

HAMMOCKS AND TOURIST TREES

Hammocks in the Everglades are not for lying in. Standing out like islands in a sea of sawgrass, they're patches of woodland growing on low outcrops of limestone which offer some firm ground where their roots will not be waterlogged. Hardwood trees such as live oak, mahogany and gumbo-limbo provide shade and shelter to many species—deer, racoon, bobcats, marsh rabbits and snakes—and nest sites for birds. The gumbo-limbo acquired the joke name of "tourist tree" from its peeling red bark, like the skin of a visitor who failed to take care against the Florida sunshine. Ouch!

to aim your visit for the drier season, between November and April, which is also better for bird-watching.

Tamiami Trail

Route US 41 runs coast to coast from Miami to Naples, cutting across the top of the Everglades. The Seminole village, now almost totally engaged in the tourist trinket business, lies alongside the highway. Nearby, a visitors' centre runs boat tours along the myriad waterways. Air boat tours are also advertised, but they have to stay outside the boundaries of the National Park—they are banned from the park itself.

Everglades National Park

An area of 560,000 ha (1,400,000 acres) of the precious wetlands is protected from development by national park status. The eastern gateway is reached by way of road 9336 from Homestead, south of Miami. Just past the park entrance, the first turn-off leads to Royal Palm Visitor Center, next to a freshwater pond called a slough (and pronounced "slew" in these parts). The shoals of garfish you can see in the shallows provide food for alligators

Something nasty surfacing through the Everglades swamp.

and herons. Boardwalks circle over the marsh and through the lush, jungle-like hammock.

Anhinga Trail

In less than 800 m (half a mile) of easy walking, the trail gives you the chance to spot an amazing range of wildlife close-up: alligators, turtles, marsh rabbits and many birds. The strange anhinga

'GATORS AND CROCS

The alligator, the best-known denizen of the Everglades, was fighting a losing battle against hunters (its skin has long been prized for shoes and handbags) and loss of habitat—as drainage schemes dried out huge areas of the wetlands before it was declared a protected species. Since then the fashion business has been supplied by increasing numbers raised on farms. As a result, the alligator has made a rapid comeback; they are off the endangered list and have been expanding their territory into (human) residential areas.

Crocodiles are a lot rarer, found only in the northeast corner of Florida Bay, and they're very shy. How do you tell the difference? The crocodile has a narrower snout, and is greenish-grey in colour instead of dark grey.

or "snakebird" swims largely underwater with its head protruding like a snake, dipping occasionally to spear a fish. Then it emerges to stand on a bush with its black wings hanging out to dry in the sun.

Flamingo

The road from Homestead ends among the mangroves on the south coast at a one-time fishing village, formerly accessible only by water. Its name resulted from a case of mistaken identity. When coloured plumes were all the rage in the late 19th century, the hunters who came to shoot roseate spoonbills for their gorgeous feathers wrongly assumed they were a kind of flamingo. The birds were threatened with extinction until they were protected by law.

These days, Flamingo is *the* centre for tours and adventure activities in the southern Everglades. You can stay at the campground or lodge, take a sightseeing cruise or a safari by all-terrain vehicle, rent a boat at the marina to go fishing, or a canoe to explore the wilderness.

Florida Bay

Between the swampy southern edge of the mainland and the long line of the Florida Keys, the shallow waters and tiny islands of the Bay make up a third of the area of Everglades National Park. Best explored in the company of a local expert, the warm waters are home to porpoise, manatee, turtle and shark, and many of the islets are the nesting sites of protected species of birds.

Western Everglades

The main western entrance to the National Park is at Everglades City, near the Gulf Coast south of Naples. It's the starting point for boat trips among the "10,000 islands", a great expanse of mangrove swamp where ospreys and bald eagles nest in the treetops. You may spot alligators, turtles, perhaps a manatee. Adventurous canoeists can take the Wilderness Waterway, 160 km (100 miles) of meandering channels through the swamps and creeks all the way to Flamingo. It takes eight days, but if you don't have that much time you can do it in 6–8 hours with the aid of an outboard motor.

THE TWO BEST CORAL REEFS Divers and snorkellers give top marks for vivid fish and colourful coral to **John Pennecamp State Park** off the northern Florida Keys, and **Looe Key Marine Sanctuary** in the Lower Keys.

Curving westward from below Miami for over 160 km (100 miles), a string of islands called the Keys (from *cayo*, Spanish for islet) is stitched together by dozens of bridges and the world's longest ocean-going road. Following the track of Henry Flagler's railroad, destroyed by a hurricane in 1935, the Overseas Highway soars and leapfrogs out to the remote old naval town of Key West, located halfway between the Florida mainland and Havana, Cuba.

Northern (Upper) Keys

The first in the chain, and the most developed, Key Largo shares its name with a Humphrey Bogart film classic, even though it wasn't made here. From another Bogart movie, the steamboat *African Queen* is moored near "Mile 100" (distances on the Keys are measured from Key West and shown on roadside markers).

John Pennekamp State Park

Snorkellers and divers come to the spectacular John Pennekamp State Park, an area of coral reef rich in tropical fish, sponges and shipwrecks. If you prefer to keep dry, try out the glass-bottomed boat which makes regular trips over the reef and permits a good view of the coral and its inhabitants.

Theater of the Sea

There's more good diving, and fishing, from Islamorada to the south, which is also the home of the long-established Theater of the Sea, a marine park with performing dolphins and sea lions. The keen young trainers here take visitors on a tour of the pools, persuading the residents to make some prodigious leaps in return for a reward of fish.

Middle Keys

Many of Henry Flagler's railway bridges between the Keys were converted to carry the Overseas Highway. In other places, you'll see sections of old bridges that have been bypassed by the modern road—they make superb fishing piers! One of the builder's most elegant achievements, Long Key Viaduct, still forms part of the road, soaring for 3 km (2 miles) from Long Key to Conch Key.

Marathon

The chief town of the Middle Keys is a crawfish fishing centre   23

Zooming off into the wide blue yonder: Florida Keys Overseas Highway.

and flourishing resort. Its museum is an excellentsource of information on local natural history and the inhabitants of the Keys from the earliest times.

Seven Mile Bridge
Beyond Marathon, Flagler's engineers faced their most daunting challenge, 11 km (7 miles) of open water. Their answer, the Seven Mile Bridge, is no longer used—a modern road bridge has replaced it—but it still stands as a memorial to the many construction workers who died in accidents during the building of the railroad, between 1905 and 1912.

Lower Keys
At their southern end, the Keys widen out into a scattered group of islands, the peaks of a largely submerged limestone shelf, rather than a single line built up from coral reefs. Most of them are well-wooded, with secluded residential areas set well back from the busy highway. The first, at the end of Seven Mile Bridge, is Bahia Honda, largely taken up by a protected state park with a lovely beach. You'll notice the unusual double-decker bridge: the roadway was added on top of the original railway bridge.

Off Looe Key, a protected area of beautiful coral reef is a magnet

24

for scuba divers (escorted groups are organized). Big Pine Key is the home of a herd of the rare Key deer, charming little animals no bigger than a large dog. Formerly hunted to the edge of extinction, they're now endangered only when they choose to wander into the path of passing traffic.

Key West

An odd mixture of people has ended up here: retired military personnel and their families, New Age health-food faddists, asthmatics in search of clean air, a black community with West Indian musical connections, writers and painters, and there's a significant gay presence. The residents are called conchs (pronounced "konks"), after the big molluscs that cling to the undersea rocks. In the same stubborn manner, before the railway or highway were built, the self-sufficient islanders lived through several hurricanes, determined not to budge despite their poor communications and isolated lifestyle.

Old Mallory Square

In the old town, Duval Street, lined with souvenir shops, restaurants and bars, ends at Old Mallory Square, scene of one of Florida's best free shows. Every evening towards sunset, a crowd gathers. Musicians, jugglers and fire-eaters entertain while the police exchange good-natured insults with the street folk.

The famous painter and naturalist John James Audubon sailed here in 1832 to paint the birds (to make the job easier, he shot them first), and it is possible that he stayed in the restored Audubon House.

SPANISH GOLD

Hidden treasure isn't just for day-dreamers and hopeful hunters wielding metal detectors. These days, it's big business. Historians estimate that over 1,600 Spanish galleons were wrecked in storms on Florida's reefs or sandbars in the 16th and 17th centuries. Sailing home from ports around the Caribbean, but especially Havana, many of them were carrying gold and silver bullion, coins and jewellery from Mexico and Peru. The ships were preyed upon by pirates too, who buried some of their booty ashore, often on the barrier islands that line the coast. Some were themselves sunk or captured before they could return to collect it. One way or another, treasure worth billions of dollars lies waiting to be discovered.

25

Traces of Hemingway

Ernest Hemingway came to Key West often and wrote several of his novels here, including *For Whom the Bell Tolls* and *To Have and Have Not*. For ten years he lived in the house (now named after him) that belonged in fact to one Captain Geiger, who furnished it with pieces salvaged from shipwrecks. Hemingway spent much of his time at a bar called Sloppy Joe's; not today's big, noisy place in Duval Street, but another in nearby Greene Street which now goes by the name of Captain Tony's Saloon.

Mel Fisher Museum

On Front Street wharf, the museum houses some of the treasure salvaged in 1985 from the wrecks of the Spanish galleons *Nuestra Señora de Atocha* and *Santa Margarita*, sunk off the coast of the Keys in a hurricane in 1622. It took Fisher's team 15 years of searching (and the loss of two divers' lives), but they eventually recovered gold coins, jewels and precious artefacts valued at over $250 million, in addition to their priceless historical interest.

Little White House

President Harry Truman used to escape to Key West for holidays in the 1940s and 50s; you can visit the attractive Little White House in the Truman Annex, an area of former naval housing beautifully redeveloped.

Fort Zachary Taylor, nearby in a small state park, was a Union stronghold in the Civil War. There's a small museum inside, and the adjacent beach is one of the island's best for swimming.

Fort Jefferson

Key West may feel like the end of the line, but Florida's tail has one more sight to offer. A short flight or a long boat trip away, 110 km (68 miles) to the west, lie the Dry Tortugas, islets long uninhabited through lack of fresh water. In 1846, one of them was chosen as the site of a great stone fortress, intended to assert US control of the shipping lanes to its Gulf ports. In spite of 30 years' work it was never finished, but it was used after the Civil War as a prison. Its most famous inmate was the unfortunate Dr Samuel Mudd, whose only "crime" was to set a broken leg, unaware that it belonged to Abraham Lincoln's fugitive assassin, John Wilkes Booth. Ignorance was deemed to be no excuse, and Mudd was given a long jail sentence. Hence the expression: "His name was mud".

No sign of Hemingway's ghost in his old back garden, but you might spot the descendants of his cats.

North of Miami, the coast is an almost unbroken line of resorts: sandy beach and palm trees facing the Atlantic breakers, stretching for more than 110 km (68 miles) to Palm Beach and beyond. Only the roadside signs reveal where one ends and the next begins.

Further north, for 440 km (274 miles) to the Georgia stateline, the density of building thins out. The holiday beaches are often on the seaward side of long, narrow offshore islands, with working towns on the mainland. Highway A1A is the scenic route, staying close to the ocean and using the islands where it can, but it is often slow going. Highway 1 is the local business route joining the towns. Anyone in a hurry uses the Interstate I-95 or Florida's Turnpike.

Fort Lauderdale

Business, banking and shipping interests don't detract from Fort Lauderdale's reputation as a fun city, and the famous training ground (or water) of many tennis and swimming stars. It sits on a maze of inland waterways with moorings for 30,000 pleasure craft: Mississippi-style paddleboats can take you on a sight-seeing trip, while on land rubber-wheeled trolley cars make tours of the town's highlights.

The Seminole Village stages alligator wrestling and runs a casino (the Seminole Indians have a degree of autonomy which exempts them from state gambling laws). On a more cultural level, The Museum of Art on Las Olas Boulevard near New River has remarkable collections of American and European contemporary art, with many paintings by the CoBrA group and a special wing devoted to the American Impressionist William Glackens, as well as Picasso ceramics and Cuban art.

Port Everglades

The oddly named Port Everglades is Fort Lauderdale's freight and cruise terminal, rivalling Miami for the big cruise-ship market to the Caribbean and the world. All-day trips leave every day for Freeport in the Bahamas, including breakfast, lunch and dinner, gambling and a show as well as an afternoon ashore.

Palm Beach

When the rich began to winter in Florida, the ultra-rich came to Palm Beach. Many still do, and enough of their palatial Italianate mansions and landscaped gardens can be seen over the clipped hedges to give an inkling of the lifestyle. Join the residents in a stroll along Worth Avenue, where elegant little shops sell the best that money can buy. The man whose railway opened up Florida, Henry Morrison Flagler, built his opulent mansion, Whitehall, in 1901. It's now a museum, with photographs and original furniture, and his private rail carriage, *The Rambler*, parked outside.

West Palm Beach, across the causeway, is less exclusive, but the Norton Gallery of Art is top class, especially in the realm of the French Impressionists.

Kennedy Space Center

Cape Canaveral was the launching site for the first American rockets to be sent into space. In 1962 astronaut John Glenn blasted off from the Cape and circled the earth three times. By 1969, when the Apollo 11 mission put Neil Armstrong and Buzz Aldrin on the moon, the Kennedy Space Center on nearby Merritt Island was in operation. In the post-cold-war world of regular Space Shuttle flights, it's still a fascinating place to discover. If you happen to be around when a launch is scheduled, you can get a relatively close look (and a deafening earful); if nothing's going up, you will be allowed to go much nearer the installations.

The Space Center shares Merritt Island with orange groves and a wildlife sanctuary: you'll see alligators basking by the roadsides and an occasional armadillo, while eagles soar overhead.

KSC Visitor Complex

The journey of discovery starts at the Visitor Complex. A 2-hour bus tour, departing every 15 minutes, is included in the admission fee and takes you to the International Space Station Center, where you can climb aboard a lifesize replica of the station, then to the LC39 Observation Gantry for a view of the launch pads and

THREE FANTASY MANSIONS Many multi-millionaires have built their dream houses in Florida, but few are open to the public. Three palaces you *can* visit: James Deering's **Villa Vizcaya** south of Miami; the Ringling's **Ca' d'Zan** at Sarasota; and Henry Flagler's **Whitehall** at Palm Beach.

The history of US rocketry displayed at the Kennedy Space Center.

the huge Vehicle Assembly Building, as well as the Apollo/ Saturn V Center, which features an authentic Saturn V rocket. Optional guided tours (best to book) are NASA Up Close, and Cape Canaveral: Then and Now.

After the tour, there's plenty to see at the Visitor Complex, from theatrical shows to an Astronaut Encounter. The Rocket Garden displays historic rockets with special lighting, and you can climb aboard Mercury, Gemini and Apollo capsules. The Astronaut Memorial, a polished granite monument, turns with the sun and reflects light on the names of 24 astronauts who died in the *Chal-*

lenger disaster or during training accidents. The IMAX films are breathtaking, projected on screens as tall as a five-storey building, in two separate theatres.

Daytona Beach

Self-proclaimed as "The World's Most Famous Beach", Daytona's 36 km (22 miles) of firm, tide-washed sand brought automobile pioneers to test and race their cars. By the 1930s, the beach saw successive world land-speed records set and broken, culminating in Sir Malcolm Campbell's 444 kph (276 mph) in 1935. The action these days has shifted inland to Daytona International

Speedway, scene of sports car, stock car and motorcycle races. Several times a year from February to July, the town is invaded by hot-rodders, black-leather clad bikers and fans. The rest of the time, it reverts to being a cheerful, unpretentious resort, popular with families—the flat sand and shallow water make it safe for small children.

St Augustine

The oldest city in the USA was founded by Spanish settlers in 1565. That was decades before the English established their colony at Jamestown, and 55 years before the voyage of the *Mayflower*. Modern St Augustine cherishes its past, and visitors are impressed to see how well it's all been preserved. Keystone of the historic town is the Castillo de San Marcos, a powerful 17th-century fortress with four corner bastions and walls too thick for cannonballs. Often attacked, the castle never fell.

On the long main thoroughfare of the old town, pedestrians-only St George Street, many little houses survive from the Spanish and British colonial eras. The Spanish Quarter Living Museum consists of restored and rebuilt homes and workshops, where locals in costume re-create the life of Spanish pioneer days with the accent on traditional crafts.

The main square, Plaza de la Constitution, has been a marketplace since the 16th century. Facing it, the Basilica Cathedral of St Augustine is largely a modern reconstruction.

St Augustine got into the tourism business in 1888 when the tycoon Henry Flagler brought the first railway to town. To accommodate well-heeled visitors from the north he built the stately Spanish-style Ponce de León Hotel, now part of Flagler College. If you have the chance, look inside the main door to see the rotunda, originally the hotel's lobby. Across the street, the Lightner Museum of 19th-century glass, musical instruments and Victoriana used to be another of Flagler's hotels, as was the nearby City Hall.

Anastasia Island

St Augustine's beaches lie a short distance away on a long, narrow island just offshore, reached by way of the Bridge of Lions over Matanzas Bay. There's a choice: you can face the sheltered waters of the bay, or head for the endless stretches of perfect sand facing the open sea. A large part of the island is designated as a state park and nature reserve, with trails through the sand dunes and salt marshes. Birdwatchers come to spot the many species of seabirds and waders.

St Augustine is as ancient as it's possible to be in the US. The "oldest wooden schoolhouse" dates from 1763.

Jacksonville

A once sleepy little southern town has now blossomed into a booming, self-confident city of 1 million people. It grew up on the winding St Johns River, which still gives shape to the city today, and was named after General Andrew Jackson, who led US troops into the region in pursuit of Seminole Indians and became Florida's first governor in 1822. A disastrous fire in 1901 levelled half the downtown area, and almost a century later, urban redevelopment has repeated the treatment. A few of the finer buildings that went up after the fire stand out amid the cleared spaces, while the glittering glass towers of big business create a new skyline along the river.

Downtown

Jacksonville Landing livens up the river front on the north side, in the heart of the downtown area. Bright shops, restaurants with open-air terraces and an international food hall line an attractive riverside walkway. Powerboats and yachts bob and weave on the water or tie up along the quay while their crews come ashore to join in the fun. Bars, nightclubs and outdoor entertainment keep the action going until late. Further west along the river, the Cummer Museum's twelve galleries trace the history of art from 2000 BC to the present day.

Just east of Jacksonville Landing, the Main Street bridge soars over the river to a park on the south bank, where the Museum of Science and History sets out successfully to entertain as well as educate.

On the southeastern outskirts, the Jacksonville Museum of Contemporary Art not only displays modern work but also some fine pre-Columbian ceramics and textiles.

Fort Caroline

On the south bank of the St Johns River, between the city and the Atlantic coast, the Fort Caroline National Memorial stands where French Huguenots arrived in 1562, only to be massacred by Spanish colonists the following year. A replica fort houses a museum with Indian artefacts and the surrounding park includes walking trails and vast wetland areas where you might spot bald eagles, turtles and manatees.

Mayport

The St Johns meets the sea at Mayport, one of the US Navy's biggest bases. Cruise liners and container ships use the modern port, and casino cruises put to sea every evening to escape Florida's restrictions on gambling. South of Mayport, beaches stretch all the way to St Augustine.

Amelia Island

First inhabited by Timuqua Indians, this barrier island has changed hands often in its time. French, Spanish and British colonizers (who named it after a daughter of King George II) were followed by the Spanish again. A spell when smugglers and pirates called the shots came to an end when US forces brought law and order in 1821.

Amelia was early into the vacation business. In the 1870s, passenger ships from New York brought the first tourist crowds ever seen in Florida, and the one-time pirates' lair of Fernandina was transformed into a pretty little Victorian town. Then Henry Flagler's railroad down the coast passed it by, carrying his clients further south. As a result, the island was largely forgotten—the reason so many 19th- and early 20th-century houses have been preserved. Now the visitors are back on its lovely beaches, its golf courses and tennis courts, but the easy-going atmosphere endures.

The seafood is excellent—at sundown, a flotilla of shrimp boats returns to Fernandina harbour bringing in the east coast's biggest catch.

33

Only a great visionary or a madman might have foretold the way the American Dream turned out in Orlando. How did a sleepy market town, far from the wheeler-dealer promoters in Miami, grow to be today's high-rise boom city? Who could have predicted that greater Orlando would have 100,000 hotel rooms and a three-runway international airport? Maybe it took an imagination like Walt Disney's to foresee how unfashionable central Florida could blossom.

Disney started buying up land southwest of Orlando in the 1960s, bit by bit and through intermediaries to avoid a speculative frenzy. The idea was to create a bigger-and-better version of the original Disneyland in California, with its own facilities and room for evolution and expansion. The Disney organization bought up 114 sq km (44 sq miles), but other entrepreneurs moved in at the fringes, sometimes with imagination and originality. New attractions ranged from Sea World, an elaborate marine park, to Universal Studios Florida, a film production centre with rides, and a score of other tourist diversions, wet and dry.

Downtown
It can't compete with the theme parks, but Orlando boasts some of its own attractions. Apart from the fabulous shopping—which they claim even men will enjoy—there are several good museums, theatre venues and music performances.

Orlando Museum of Art
Set in Lock Haven Park, north of town, the museum's highlight is its pre-Columbian Gallery, featuring the arts of Central and South America from 1200 BC to AD 1500. Some of the finest known examples of Peruvian pottery, textiles and goldwork are beautifully displayed. For young visitors there's a hands-on art exhibit called Art Encounter. Nearby are the Orange County Historical Museum and the Orlando Science Center. The Charles Hosmer Morse Museum of American Art displays a fine collection of stained glass designed by Louis Comfort Tiffany.

Walt Disney World Resort
Not just one theme park, but four, plus aquatic parks, golf courses, dozens of hotels, countless restau-

34

rants and shops make up the most popular tourist attraction on earth.

In the beginning there was the Magic Kingdom Park, opened in 1971. EPCOT followed in 1982, intended to educate as well as entertain. Then they transplanted a chunk of Hollywood to Central Florida with the Disney-MGM Studios, topped in 1998 by the innovative Animal Kingdom Theme Park, juxtaposing real and imaginary creatures.

Magic Kingdom Theme Park

Seven different "lands" make up this fantasy world as seen through the eyes of Disney's image-makers. *Main Street, USA* depicts life as it might have been in a small country town somewhere in middle-America in

Are they for real? In the Animal Kingdom you have to look twice.

the year 1900. The street leads to the Plaza, the hub of the park, where the landmark *Cinderella Castle*, 55 m (180 ft) high, dwarfs the one in California.

Adventureland goes to some exotic locations—the Amazon, a mystical Asia and the pirate-infested Caribbean. *Frontierland* commemorates the Wild West in story and song and adventurous rides, most hair-raisingly Splash Mountain. Liberty Square isn't all flag-waving, but the Hall of Pres-

idents does bring on lifelike animated figures of every US president.

Fantasyland is a favourite with the very young, with gentle, old-fashioned fairground rides, some based on Disney characters. *Mickey's Starland* is dedicated to the original mouse himself. *Tomorrowland* is equipped with futuristic rides, notably *Space Mountain*, a stomach-churning roller-coaster trip through pitch

WALT'S RAILROAD

Once through the gates of the Magic Kingdom, you'll pass under the railway that runs right round its borders. The old-fashioned trains are drawn by real steam engines, built between 1916 and 1928 and found working in Mexico's Yucatan peninsula in the 1960s. Rebuilt to pristine perfection, they were given the names *Walter E. Disney*, *Lilly Belle* (after Walt's wife), *Roy O. Disney* and *Roger Broggie* (one of Walt Disney's "imagineers" and a fellow railroad buff). A ride in an open carriage gives you a fabulous tour through bamboo thickets, jungles and forests and past real-looking old-timers and Native Americans. You can get on or off at Frontierland or Mickey's Starland, and at the main entrance.

darkness. A fearsome experience awaits with the *Extraterrorestrial Alien Encounter*, where you are trapped in a dark room with a murderous alien.

EPCOT

The Experimental Prototype Community of Tomorrow, shortened to EPCOT, comes in two distinct parts, laid out like the circles of a figure 8.

Next to the main gate, *Future World* features the wonders of science and technology. The central landmark is a big white "geosphere" called *Spaceship Earth*, a ride as well as a sight. Around it, the twin buildings of Communi-Core East and West set out to enlighten you about computers, communications and robotics. Then comes an outer ring of seven pavilions, each sponsored by a giant of American industry —all entertaining and informative, with rides, interactive exhibits, 3D and laser shows. Nowadays there's increasing emphasis on safeguarding the environment.

The southern half of EPCOT, World Showcase, groups various national pavilions around a big lagoon, each sponsored by a country. They don't shrink from employing every cliché to promote themselves, but in very different ways.

EPCOT's *IllumiNations* fills the sky with fireworks and crisscrossing laser beams. The World Showcase buildings are lit up and water fountains play, accompanied by synchronized music. Anywhere around World Showcase can make a good vantage point for EPCOT shows, but seats tend to be taken early, especially in the waterside eating places.

Disney-MGM Studios

Real and simulated movie sets are only part of the story in this park designed to look like 1930s Hollywood. Even the eating places are "themed", with period decor and costumed staff. Besides backstage tours, revelations of special effects and the intricacies of cartoon animation, there are rides and films relating to historic and recent Disney productions, including an all-singing, all-dancing musical at the Theater of the Stars. Not all the attractions are derived from Disney originals— one spectacular show is based on some of the stunts used in the film adventures of Indiana Jones.

TV shows and movies inspire a number of rides, one of the scariest involving a runaway elevator in the *Twilight Zone Tower of Terror*, which drops you 13 storeys in a couple of seconds (faster than gravity)—over and over again. The *Rock'n' Roller Coaster starring Aerosmith* pro-

THEME PARK TIPS

- Dress is casual, but bare feet and bare chests are banned.
- There's a lot of walking and standing, so wear your most comfortable shoes.
- You are not permitted to take your own food and drink into the theme parks. There are plenty of places to eat inside.
- Arrive early—before the gates open—to beat the crowds. Study the free map each park provides.
- Leave any shopping until after you have taken some rides.
- If you want to go out and come back (even to go to the car park), have your hand stamped at the exit, and carry your ticket.
- Take in some cash for fast food and drinks. Only sit-down restaurants accept credit cards.
- Smoking isn't allowed in the attractions, or in the queues and waiting areas. Restaurants have smoking and non-smoking sections.
- Flash photography is not permitted in most attractions.

pels you from 0 to 60 mph in 2.8 seconds, then loops, whirls and corkscrews to the beat of the famous group's music.

Animal Kingdom Theme Park

The centrepiece of Disney's latest theme park on animal life is *The Tree of Life* on Discovery Island. The artificial tree is made up of some 300 ingeniously carved animals. No creature is too insignificant to be considered, as you'll see from the 3D animated film, *It's Tough to Be a Bug.*

Bigger game is on view in *Africa*, which you reach through the village of Harambe. Here, with Kilimanjaro Safaris, you board a Land Rover to meander through the African savannah. Pangan Forest Exploration Trail is a research centre filled with more exotic animals.

In *Asia*, you can challenge the Kali River Rapids on a raft, join the Maharajah Jungle Trek to explore the ruins of an ancient Indian palace where tigers, giant fruit bats and Komodo dragons lurk, or watch the birds in Flights of Wonder.

Dinoland USA is full of rollercoasters on a dinosaur theme, while *Rafiki's Planet Watch* includes a Conservation Station where you can see how wild animals are cared for, and an Affection Section for stroking cuddly creatures.

There's more entertainment, parades and shows at *Camp Minnie-Mickey* and the *Oasis* (watch out for those giant anteaters).

Blizzard Beach Water Park

On the western side of Walt Disney World, Blizzard Beach was supposedly created by a freak winter storm that left a ski resort in its wake. Mt Gushmore is the pivot of this water adventure park; you can ride to the top and plummet down its almost vertical slopes on a toboggan. People love it: get there early. If it sounds too terrifying for you, try floating on an inner tube through Runoff Rapids, slalom through the Snow Stormers or try rock-climbing—face the Slush and Climb Mt Gush!

Lake Buena Vista

Grouped around a lagoon are several hotels and self-contained resorts, not forgetting the famous Lake Buena Vista golf course.

Take your swimwear to Typhoon Lagoon Water Park to sample its elaborate water slides, its rubber-rafting thrills on whitewater rapids, body-surfing in waves generated by machine, and snorkelling above an artificial coral reef.

Pleasure Island, the nightlife district, is designed to discourage Walt Disney World fun-lovers from straying off campus after dark. It's set in a clever pastiche of an old fishing port, complete with ramshackle warehouses turned into a variety of venues, including some distinctive restaurants, shops and bars. Around midnight, the streets become the stage for a party, and live music, dancing and entertainment go on until about 2 a.m.

Sea World

The biggest of Florida's marine life parks stars the friendly killer whale Shamu, who splashes the front-row spectators with sea water. Dolphins and sea lions do their tricks in exchange for handouts of fish, although it really does seem as if they're enjoying themselves too.

Manatee Rescue is a lush lagoon inhabited by endangered sea cows, which you can see from above and below. In Shark Encounter, you can walk through the world's largest transparent tunnel, surrounded by sharks of all sizes, eels, barracuda and menacing fish with venomous stings. On a humid Florida day, you may envy the penguins: the natural comedians of the Antarctic live in a refrigerated tank furnished with machine-made snow, while Base Station Wild Arctic shows you what life is like in the land of polar bears, walruses, beluga whales and seals, all at home here in their man-made ocean.

Humans provide some of the entertainment at SeaWorld, with water-ski shows on the park's big lake. The white-knuckle *Kraken* ride turns you upside down seven times and is reputedly the best rollercoaster in the Orlando area.

In the adjacent Discovery Cove, you can swim alongside stingrays and dolphins.

Wet'n'Wild

Like Disney's Typhoon Lagoon, this aquapark has a giant wave-

4

FOUR DOWNTOWN REVIVALS Many
American cities have created bright new entertainment, eating and shopping areas to attract people back to the city centre. Some of the most successful: the food outlets and boutiques of Miami's **Bayside Marketplace**; the **Bayfront Center** on St Petersburg's waterfront; Tampa's **Ybor City** area of former cigar factories; and the riverside walkway, bars and restaurants of **Jacksonville Landing**.

Dolphins jump for joy in Sea World while Shamu the killer whale keeps a low profile.

machine and plenty of water-slides. Thrill-seekers can plunge nearly vertically down a 23-m (75-ft) slide in *Bomb Bay* or slide through the tubes of 6-storey-high *Blue Niagra*.

Universal Orlando

This huge complex between Walt Disney World and Orlando incorporates several hotels and resorts, together with a dining, shopping and entertainment centre, City Walk, the theme park Islands of Adventure, and Universal Studios Florida, an ambitious combination of theme park and working film and TV production facility.

Islands of Adventure

Universal's first "non-studio" theme park opened in 1999. Its state-of-the-art rides are grouped on five different "islands", aimed at different age-groups. Several hair-raising adventures await in *Jurassic Park;* while on *The Lost Continent* you can board two stomach-churning roller-coasters, *Dueling Dragons – Fire* and *Dueling Dragons – Ice*, or try to escape from *Poseidon's Fury* as the warring gods hurl giant fire-balls at you. But the general consensus is that the most thrilling ride of all is *The Amazing Adventures of Spider-Man,* on Marvel Super Hero Island, where you may also like to contend with the *Incredible Hulk.*

Universal Studios Florida

Covering 444 acres (180 ha), this capitalizes on past hits with the *Back to the Future* simulator-ride, surrounding the audience with a 360° screen while throwing them around in DeLorean cars; *Revenge of the Mummy*, a ride in total darkness where you confront fireballs, scarab beetles and an army of warrior mummies; and *Twister: Ride it Out,* where you get caught in the vortex of a tornado. The sinister-sounding *Men in Black: Alien Attack* is based on the hit movie. If you're feeling philanthropic you can save the human race from extermination by nasty cyborgs in *Terminator 2: 3-D Battle Across Time. Shrek 4-D* is a 3-D film enhanced by special effects where you feel the action right in your seat. Children flock to *Woody Woodpecker's Kidzone*, packed with hands-on entertainment, and everyone loves to ride in the sky on a bicycle in *E.T. Adventure.*

Kissimmee

This charmingly named cattle-town south of Orlando has been all but submerged by the Disney-led tourist explosion. Kissimmee's own bid for tourist attention is Splendid China, a 30-ha

(74-acre) theme park with miniature replicas of more than 60 of the wonders of China. The Great Wall has been reduced to half a mile, using about 6 million tiny bricks.

Gatorland was a pioneer attraction, opened soon after World War II. Its main function is to breed alligators for their skins, but some of the 5,000 reptiles in residence also take part in the entertainment business. Feeding time is compulsive viewing, and there's an 800-seat stadium to accommodate fans of alligator wrestling (man against beast). You can buy an alligator-hide belt, billfold or handbag, and even snack on deep-fried alligator chunks.

Cypress Gardens

South of Orlando near Winter Haven, this lakeside park has been pulling in the crowds since it opened as a botanic garden in 1936. Its lake was soon taken over by the new sport of water-skiing, with ever more spectacular shows staged for visitors. They've become more artistic and ambitious every year. Low-speed electric boat trips through the gardens show off many of the 8,000 species of plants, and other attractions include a simulated Florida town of around 1900 and a conservatory inhabited by free-flying butterflies.

Tourism was slower to develop on the side of Florida facing the Gulf of Mexico, which never seemed to attract as much attention as the Atlantic coast. It had its admirers—northerners including Henry Ford and Thomas Edison built winter homes here a century ago—but Miami and Palm Beach grabbed the publicity. Now all that has changed. First American, then European vacationers discovered the warm, sheltered waters and gently sloping beaches of white sand, the sailing, fishing and golf.

Tampa

Florida's third-biggest city has a chequered past, with long empty spaces in its recorded history. When the Spanish conquistador Hernando de Soto landed, his reception by local Indians was so hostile that he scratched the area from his colonization list. In fact, the Indians had the place to themselves until 1823, when the United States army put its foot down and established Fort Brooke. Not until late in the 19th century was the river dredged to transform Tampa into a real port. At the same period, the railway arrived, joining Tampa to the rest of Florida and points north.

Tourism descended on Tampa in 1889 with the construction of the outrageously opulent Tampa Bay Hotel. The brain behind it was the man who brought the railway to the Gulf, Henry Plant. His idea was to fill the hotel in winter and empty it during summer's heat—unwittingly assuring its dilapidation. Plant died before the domed, doomed hotel hit the skids. The city turned it over to the University of Tampa, whose undergraduates convene in the former lobby during their leisure hours. The public is offered guided tours of the bizarre building; part is a museum commemo-

5 **FIVE THEME PARK THRILLS** Try Walt Disney World's **Space Mountain** roller-coaster hurtling through pitch darkness and the **Splash Mountain** rush down a waterfall, and Universal Studios' **Back to the Future** all-enveloping virtual reality ride. At Busch Gardens Tampa don't miss the duelling **Gwazi** roller-coaster and the **Kumba** with its vertical loop.

rating Plant's era. Another cultural high spot, the Tampa Museum of Art on the riverbank is known for its antiquities as well as contemporary American art.

Ybor City

For a few decades, this Tampa suburb was the scene of an extraordinary boom: cigars. The tobacco leaves were shipped in from Cuba; the workers, too. Production began in 1886 and before long there were 200 factories. Tampa became the "Cigar Capital of the World". But then the fashion switched to cigarettes, and cigars were to prove a vulnerable luxury when the Great Depression struck in the 1930s.

The area along 7th and 8th Avenues, from 13th Street to 22nd Street, has retained much of the atmosphere of a century ago. Some of the factories have found new uses; among the little shops and bars you'll find antique shops and restaurants—and you can still buy handmade cigars. Ybor City State Museum on 9th Avenue documents the cigar town's history and the strong Cuban connection, which is a couple of generations older than Miami's.

Busch Gardens

The giant brewing corporation, Anheuser-Busch, runs a massive theme park northeast of Tampa. The setting is Africa: many of the buildings look like old Timbuktu. Big game animals roam the "Serengeti" plain—you view them from the safety of a cablecar, a monorail or a romantic oldfashioned steam train. An ice show breaks the African pattern, and riders on the *Kumba* rollercoaster hardly know *where* they are—it's the longest, fastest and tallest in all Florida. The double *Gwazi* isn't bad either, with close encounters between the lion and tiger rides. You can tour the onsite brewery, and adults can sample some of the beers.

St Petersburg

The other St Petersburg, the one in Russia, might seem to have little in common with a warm, sunny retirement haven, but the Florida version does have some cultural pretensions of its own. The town adjoins Tampa Bay, signalling its presence with a pastel-coloured pier shaped like an inverted pyramid. Its beaches are quite separate, some way to the west facing the Gulf.

Salvador Dalí Museum

A vast collection of the Catalan surrealist's work came to "St Pete" by courtesy of a collector from Cleveland who got to know Dalí in the 1940s. The museum has so many of his paintings, drawings and sculptures that it may be useful to take one of the   43 guided tours of the highlights. That way, you can avoid becoming swamped, and will be able to put into perspective the career of the genius with the upswept moustaches, who declared himself the World's Greatest Painter.

Fine Arts Museum

After an overdose of Dalí, a small but varied collection makes a refreshing change. Housed in a mansion on the street leading to the pier, it features works by Georgia O'Keeffe, Grandma Moses and James Whistler as well as French Impressionists.

Pinellas Suncoast

From St Petersburg Beach north to Clearwater, a 32-km (20-mile) string of barrier islands lies just offshore. Linked to each other and the mainland by bridges and causeways, they form one long strip of holiday homes, hotels and motels. There's the usual Florida profusion of places to eat, from bargain buffets to more expensive seafood restaurants. Some of the beaches are superb, and the crimson and purple sunsets can be spell-binding.

Sarasota

The cultural capital of the west coast has its own orchestra, and puts on winter seasons of ballet, theatre and opera in a futuristic pink and purple auditorium. Downtown, old shops have been restored and outdoor cafés and restaurants, some with live entertainment, take advantage of warm evenings. Jungle and orchid gardens, a bird sanctuary and an aquarium are among other diversions, and Bellm's Cars and Music of Yesterday displays huge collections of classic vehicles and every sort of mechanical musical instrument, from tiny musical boxes to giant fairground organs.

SPONGEORAMA

What a name! But for a comprehensive briefing on sponge-diving and the deep-sea creatures concerned, this is the place—Spongeorama in Tarpon Springs. The town, north of Clearwater, was developed at the beginning of the 20th century by Greek divers. By holding their breath for minutes at a time, they could bring up masses of the skeletons so prized in the world's bathrooms. Competition from synthetic sponges later cut into the business, but a few divers are still at work (equipped with air tanks these days). The main activity of the port now is fishing, especially for shrimp. Tarpon Springs takes it name from the tarpon, a bony flying fish that grows to an impressive size in the Gulf waters.

Two barrier islands joined by causeways to the town, Lido Key and Siesta Key, provide sparkling white sand beaches where the local residents and winter vacationers go to relax, jog, swim and fly kites.

The Ringling House and Museums

The name of Sarasota is forever linked with that of Ringling— as in Ringling Brothers Circus. John Ringling, its co-founder, started as a clown but eventually amassed a fortune, having bought the rival Barnum and Bailey Circus and merged it with his own. In the 1920s, he and his wife Mable settled down in northern Sarasota, the winter quarters of his circus, and proceeded to build their dream house. Ca' d'Zan ("John's House" in Venetian dialect) is a Gothic mansion in Venetian style, tastefully designed and furnished. The Ringlings' art collection, more than 700 works by the likes of Rubens, Rembrandt, Cranach, Van Dyck and Veronese, outgrew the house, and a magnificent museum in the shape of a Renaissance palace was built in the grounds to house them.

Also in the compound is the Circus Museum, with posters, costumes, props and wagons, evoking the great days of the touring circus and its stars, such as "General" Tom Thumb, only 70 cm (28 in) tall, and his bad-tempered, equally diminutive wife Lavinia. Near the museum is the little Asolo Theater, a jewel of Italian rococo architecture dating from 1728. It stood in Asolo, northwest of Venice, until John Ringling bought it and had it dismantled piece by piece and brought to Florida. It was rebuilt here in 1950, and now serves as a conservatory for drama students, who stage frequent performances.

Fort Myers

On the banks of the Caloosahatchee River, Fort Myers was one of the first places in Florida to catch the eye of northerners looking for a warm place to spend the winter. Now it is a fast-expanding commercial centre, and the uncrowded Gulf Coast beaches a short drive away are beginning to be discovered.

Inland, cattle graze on pastures created a century ago by draining wetlands and clearing some of the big cypress trees. You can tour the vast Babcock Wilderness Ranch, six times the size of Manhattan, on open safari wagons, spotting alligators, rattlesnakes and the varied birdlife among the swamps and forests.

The Edison Winter Home

The inventor Thomas Alva Edison (1847–1931) fled to Fort 45

Myers when winter snows up north affected his health, but he kept on working. His house at 2350 McGregor Boulevard includes his study and a laboratory he built, as well as an exotic garden. (He was trying to find an alternative source of natural rubber.) A museum displays the breadth of his genius—he invented not only the electric light bulb, but also the stock-market ticker, the microphone, the phonograph and scores of other useful things. Edison's friend Henry Ford built a house next door, also open to visitors.

Sanibel and Captiva

Two fashionable little offshore islands long ago attracted the wealthy in search of the simple life. Even now that they are linked by a long causeway to the mainland near Fort Myers, and by a bridge to each other, they have retained their exclusivity. Although there's a lot more holiday traffic than the residents would like, overbuilding and exploitation have been resisted. The south shore is ringed by sands which collect a harvest of shells from sea currents sweeping north up the Gulf Coast. Serious

Ca' d'Zan: Venetian name for the Gothic mansion of circus owner John Ringling.

collectors and amateurs alike bend earnestly over the shallows in search of the finest specimens. (Make sure you don't take any live ones!)

The north side of the island, facing Pine Island Sound, is a designated wildlife refuge, an area of mangrove swamp and shallow bays, the natural habitat of wading birds. You can drive through part of it, but of course it's far better for the environment if you take the time to walk, or rent a bicycle and pedal yourself along.

Naples

In the Gulf Coast's most exclusive town, elegant homes line a network of waterways—boat tours give inquisitive visitors a close look. Even the fashionable shopping mall is like a little Venice. The long beach is renowned for its shells, and every dawn and low tide brings out collectors. A teddy bear museum and big game park add to the variety, and not far away inland, Corkscrew Swamp Sanctuary is a remnant of the forests of bald cypress (so-called because they drop their leaves in winter) which once covered great tracts of south-west Florida. A number of these giant survivors tower 40 m (130 ft) into the sky; tree-ring dating has shown some of them to be over 700 years old.

47

Stretching west along the Gulf of Mexico, Florida takes in a slice of land that geographical logic might have given to Alabama. Foreigners and even some Floridians tend to forget that this is part of the "Sunshine State", and indeed the atmosphere is more like its Deep South neighbours. Yet it contains the state capital, Tallahassee, and the busy port of Pensacola, far older than Miami or Jacksonville.

Tallahassee

Set in gently rolling hill country (untypical of the Florida peninsula), Tallahassee is a rather quiet city whose centre is dominated by the New Capitol Building and the bureaucrats who work there. Livening things up in term time are the tens of thousands of students who attend Florida State University. For an understanding of the state's convoluted past, visit the Museum of Florida History, the best of its kind.

Panama City

Florida's Panama is a brash, cheerful, commercial resort, a strip of motels, bars and amusement parks, with a vast beach of soft white sand stretching more than 40 km (25 miles). Unlike most of the state, high season here is the summer, with another peak at "spring break", when students pour in from the cold north intent on an endless party.

Pensacola

At the far western end of the Panhandle, only a short half-day's drive from New Orleans, Pensacola was an early Spanish settlement, later seized by the French and then the British. Spain grabbed it back during the American War of Independence and then ceded it to the new United States along with the rest of Florida in 1821. The six blocks of Historic Pensacola Village preserve some of the houses of that time. The US Navy has one of its main air bases here, and fans of old aircraft must not miss the National Museum of Naval Aviation—the NC-4 flying boat on display was the first plane to fly the Atlantic (stopping in the Azores on the way).

Offshore barrier islands offer all the sand, blue sea and water-sports you could wish, as well as the beautiful Gulf Islands nature reserve. Fort Pickens on Santa Rosa Island held out for the Union during the Civil War. Afterwards, the Native American hero Geronimo was imprisoned there.

Cultural Notes

Culture Vultures

After the famous financiers and industrialists piled up their vast fortunes, many of them turned to culture, building libraries, funding museums and galleries, and filling them with art. Some of these bigtime collectors were hoodwinked into paying heavily for fakes and works of dubious attribution, but others skimmed the cream of Europe, often buying from impoverished aristocrats.

The tradition of giving to museums, or even endowing new ones, still continues, and the donors often lay down strict conditions about display. If one city doesn't agree to their terms, another will get the treasures. You'll see the benefits of such generosity all over Florida: among them, the Ringlings' Old Master paintings at Sarasota; the Norton Gallery at West Palm Beach, the Morse Museum of art nouveau glass at Winter Park, and the Reynolds and Morse collection of the work of Salvador Dalí at St Petersburg.

Performing Arts

Well-heeled winter vacationers supported live theatre in the old days, and now it's back again. Touring productions, pre- and post-Broadway, and revivals come to Miami Beach, Coconut Grove, Palm Beach, Fort Lauderdale and Sarasota.

Miami is big and bold enough to support the Florida Grand Opera and Miami City Ballet, as well as its own symphony orchestra. Sarasota puts in a claim to be cultural capital of the state. Its Van Wezel Hall hosts a season of opera, ballet, concerts and plays, mainly by visiting companies, and a spring Jazz Festival.

Popular Music

The 20th was an American century. Movement after movement exploded and evolved, spawning ever more variations. Ragtime and blues led to jazz, in all its incarnations, and jazz influenced every other sort of music from hit songs to the avant garde. And they all sounded unmistakably American, although jazz had its roots in African rhythms, and some of the most successful writers of popular music—George Gershwin, Irving Berlin—came from eastern Europe.

Country and western, rhythm'n' blues, rock'n'roll, heavy metal, soul and rap have been copied everywhere, but the originals are stamped "Made in the USA".

49

Shopping

The United States is truly the land where you can "shop till you drop". The range of goods is astonishing, consumer protection laws ensure that customers' interests are paramount, and sales staff have a refreshingly positive, "can-do" attitude. Competition keeps prices down and there always seems to be some sort of sale going on somewhere—check out the Friday and Sunday editions of local newspapers. When you are comparing prices, be prepared for the addition of a local sales tax of about 6 per cent. And remember that when you arrive home, you are legally required to declare any substantial purchases and may be charged import duty and VAT.

Where to Shop

The modern mode of shopping is the mall. Department stores, famous-name designer boutiques and little speciality shops are enclosed in a climate-controlled space. Plenty of eating places are available too. In this age of the automobile, some of the biggest malls are far from city centres, but close to major highways and with parking lots the size of airports.

Large supermarkets can supply most basic needs. They stock much more than food, just as drug stores sell much more than medicinal supplies. Enquire at the tourist information offices about farmers' markets and other traditional markets too.

For quality gifts and souvenirs, a reproduction art work or just some beautiful postcards, look in the shops run by the museums and art galleries. Some of them have a fine range of books too, not necessarily restricted to the museum's own field.

Clothes

Every designer in the world seems to be represented, with a good chance of finding just what you want at a price lower than in its country of origin. The latest fashions quickly appear as ready-to-wear, and just as quickly go on sale at big discounts before the season is half over. The US leads the way in stylish casual clothing and sportswear.

Prices can vary enormously from store to store: a swimsuit in a seafront hotel's boutique may be four times the cost of an identical one in a department store not far away. So-called "factory outlets" on the edges of towns or out along the freeways may charge even less, for surplus lines and last year's models—great for stocking up on jeans.

Jewellery

You could spend a king's ransom in the top Palm Beach jewellers, but there's an incredible range of beautiful work at more accessible prices too. Look for unusual local stones, which may not be particularly valuable but rank high in novelty appeal. Costume jewellery, especially in the mall boutiques, can be the best buy: some designs are brilliantly innovative and very inexpensive.

Gadgets

The endless American quest to make things easier, be it in the garage, the kitchen or the bathroom, means there is a range of tricks and tools you can find nowhere else in the world. Take a look in the stationery and office supply stores such as Staples for bright ideas at low prices.

Electronics

The latest computer, hi-fi and video equipment is available at competitive prices, but there are several pitfalls for the unwary. Make sure you are not being sold last year's model at this year's price; and check that the electrical supply and other factors are compatible with those in your home country. It is best to go to a large, approved dealer and obtain a world-wide guarantee.

Books, CDs and DVDs

With their vast selections and reasonable prices the bookstores are a pleasure to browse around. Discounting is normal practice.

Every sort of music can be found on CD, with frequent price wars as an incentive to buy. They'll work on European players, *unlike* pre-recorded videotapes, which operate on a different system unless specially made for export. DVDs are for Zone 1.

Crafts and Antiques

Most of what is sold as craftwork is mass-produced and imported, but it is worth looking for the rare creative pieces. By all means visit the antique shops, although you may be shocked by the prices.

Flea markets, often claiming to be the biggest in the state, are widely advertised in weekend papers and along highways. Don't expect to make any great finds, but you can have fun among the second-hand goods, rejects, bygones and junk.

Dining Out

Newcomers will be amazed by the sheer number and variety of eating places. Where a European town might have ten, somewhere the same size in the US will have a hundred: steak houses, fast food outlets and restaurants including a dozen different ethnic variations. Such hot competition is a fair assurance of value for money and cheerful, efficient service. It comes as no surprise that the average American eats out four or five times a week.

Breakfast

The eating day begins with the offer of coffee before you've even looked at the menu. Main dishes include eggs "any style" and waffles or pancakes with butter and maple syrup. With any of these you can order bacon, ham, spicy sausage and hash browns (grated potato, fried until crisp). Sweet rolls and "Danish" (sweet pastries) are the typical local accompaniment. If you prefer toast—white, wholewheat or rye bread—ask for it; specify "dry" if you don't want it pre-buttered.

Salads

Many restaurants have do-it-yourself salad bars, simple or elaborate, with raw vegetables, fresh fruit, even seafood, cold meats and cheeses.

Salad dishes from the menu can be enormous, enough for a meal on their own. A smaller salad may be included in the price of the main course, although it will be brought first, with a choice of dressing.

Fish and shellfish

Southern waters are great for grouper, red snapper, yellowtail, at their best simply broiled (grilled) and served with a lemon and butter sauce. Catfish is a bewhiskered native of freshwater creeks and rivers, and now also farmed. As well as lobsters and oysters from all along the east coast, the shellfish menu offers crabs, scallops, shrimp and crawfish. Stone crabs, a seasonal delicacy, are complicated to eat but well worth the trouble.

Meat

For red meat eaters, the steaks are outsized, tender and tasty, and the

roast prime rib of beef is a revelation. Try one of the chains that specialize in steaks, such as Outback or the quality Ruth's Chris Steak Houses. Barbecued spare (pork) ribs are mighty tasty, and it's entirely proper to eat them with your fingers.

Ethnic variations

The choice used to be limited to Italian, Mexican and Chinese, all tailored to American tastes, which often meant toning down the flavours. Now there is greater authenticity, and a range as diverse as the population. Few towns are without a Thai restaurant, and many have Vietnamese, Japanese and Indian too. Big cities boast Afghan, Russian, Greek and many more, plus British and Irish pubs.

In Miami, the big Cuban community ensures good *picadillo* (marinated ground beef mixed with olives, green peppers, garlic, onions and tomato sauce) and *arroz con pollo* (chicken and rice), and potent coffee, otherwise a rarity in the USA.

Desserts and cheeses

The American sweet tooth is seduced by sugary pecan pie, or meringue-topped Key lime pie (referring to the Florida Keys, but the pie travels well). As for ice cream, the Americans really do excel, with a thousand and one flavours you didn't even know existed and calorific toppings. Frozen yoghurt is a delicious, diet-conscious alternative.

Drinks

Fresh fruit juices are pure pleasure, whether from local oranges or something more exotic. Other non-alcoholic choices include the American favourite, iced tea, and the ubiquitous international soft drink brands.

You must be 21 or over to buy alcoholic drinks, or to consume them in public. The selection of wines is as wide as you might find anywhere: imports from all over the world compete with the products of several American states. The custom is to identify wine by the grape variety or combination of varieties used: Cabernet sauvignon, Pinot Noir and Zinfandel, for example, in the reds; Sauvignon Blanc and Chardonnay in the whites. Rosé wines are often called "blush" here.

American beers are becoming more varied and interesting, with the growth of local brands and a fashion for micro-breweries. "Light" (or Lite) means low-calorie, not low-alcohol. Domestic or imported, beer is always served ice cold. Spirits (called liquor) are normally served with loads of ice, whether "on the rocks" or accompanied by a mixer. A final note: bar staff expect to be tipped.

Sports

Florida's busiest time is the winter, when it's usually ideal for golf and tennis and the seas are still warm enough for swimming, but sun-loving Europeans have extended the season to last the whole year. Any time, anywhere, you can join the local legions of joggers and walkers, rent a bicycle or try the fastest-growing style of self-propulsion, roller-blading.

Water Sports

Chains of offshore islands protect a lot of the coast, so you often have a choice between sheltered waters and the open sea. The calmer stretches are perfect for learning to waterski or windsurf: most resorts have sailboards for rent. Beaches can be vast and it's easy to escape the crowds, but if you have any doubts about swimming, stick to the popular areas where lifeguards keep watch and post warning signs when necessary.

The Florida Keys are great for snorkelling among reef fish. Scuba-diving centres hire equipment and run trips to some of the best sites. You need a certified diver's card to go independently, but many centres offer classes to take you to that standard.

It's an American dream to own a boat: better still is to live next to the water so you can embark at your front door. Up and down the coast, inlets and creeks are a forest of masts, and Florida has a maze of inland waterways, perfect for a leisurely sail. All sorts of craft can be hired, from simple dinghies to floating palaces.

Fishing

Whether in lakes or bayous, casting from open beaches or going after the big ones offshore, fishing is a national passion. You can rent rods and reels, and the US is a good place to buy equipment. Bait shops will advise on what to fish for, and they will tell you if licences are needed. If you want to go deep-sea fishing for marlin, shark or tuna, talk to some of the captains with boats for hire: you'll find them at most of the big marinas.

Golf

Nowhere in the world is better provided with golf courses. Florida has over a thousand, and 55 no matter where you are, you won't be far from a course. Many big resort hotels have their own and Walt Disney World has a handful. They're typically in picture-book condition, manicured to perfection (Americans don't even like the rough to be untidy). Many of them welcome visitors and in general, fees are reasonable, although some places make it compulsory to rent and use a ride-on buggy. If you aspire to play one of the famous courses which host the big championships, reserve well in advance and be prepared to pay a lot more. For some of the more exclusive clubs, you may need an introduction.

Tennis

Many hotels have courts, especially the big resorts which also offer coaching and equipment rental. (Compare the prices at the sports departments of the big stores too; it could be worth buying what you need.) If you play early or late you can avoid the summer heat: you may be able to take advantage of the floodlighting that is often provided—for an additional fee.

Spectator Sports

Television stirs up interest in practically any form of sport, provided a US team or player is involved. But for as long as anyone can remember, the truly national games have been baseball and American football, closely followed by basketball and hockey (ice hockey, that is—the kind played on grass is called field hockey). They are the ones that get the fans screaming and the kids dressing in the uniforms of their idols.

Any big city worth its salt wants to have its own Major League (first division) teams. In football, Miami has its Dolphins, Tampa Bay its Buccaneers, and Jacksonville was over the moon when its new Jaguars were accepted into the National Football League in 1995. Orlando Magic and Miami Heat jumped to prominence on the national basketball scene in the 1980s and have stayed there ever since. As well as self-respect, vast sums of money are involved. The teams are run like corporations, bought and sold and even enticed away from one city by another.

Florida's weather makes it an out-of-season base for baseball, football and other teams, who put on practice games that are open to spectators. There's nearly always a big tennis or golf tournament going on somewhere, together with horse-racing and the Hispanic favourite, *jai alai*. This high-speed indoor sport is a blend of squash and lacrosse, pronounced "high lie".

The Hard Facts

Airports

International gateway airports include Miami, Orlando and Tampa. In the passenger terminals you'll find currency exchanges, bars and restaurants, duty-free shops for departing international passengers, gift shops, car rental and hotel reservation desks and tourist information offices.

There is generally a transportation desk where you can ask about ways to get to the city, your hotel or other local destinations. Some hotels run free shuttle buses. There may be a "limo" (often a minibus) serving a number of hotels, or an airport bus to a downtown terminal, and taxis are always available. For all of these, pick-up points are marked by signs outside the arrivals building.

Check-in for international flights is generally at least an hour before the flight time. But airlines suggest you come two hours ahead, to ensure you get the seat you want, and to allow for security procedures. Early check-in also reduces the chance of being "bumped" (refused a seat, even though confirmed, and put on a later flight). If it happens, you are entitled to compensation under US law.

Baggage

On most transatlantic flights, you are allowed to check in two pieces of baggage per person, with no weight restriction. One carry-on bag is permitted. Take any medicines you may need—the same brands may not be available, or only on prescription.

Car Rental

Hiring a car is the most convenient way of getting around, and often the most economical. It pays to shop around for deals. There can be a considerable price advantage in making a reservation in your home country, well before your visit. Check that rates include full insurance against damage (CDW: collision damage waiver). There is normally no charge for distance travelled, but be prepared for extra charges for an additional driver, drop-off at a different location and local taxes.

To rent a car, you need to hold a current driving licence and to be over 21 (25 with some companies). There may be an upper age limit of 70. You are expected to pay with a major credit card: it is normal for the rental company to charge the estimated cost of the rental in advance and adjust the amount if necessary when you return the car.

For added security and convenience, many agencies offer a mobile phone with the car for a surprisingly small extra charge.

Climate
Winter in south Florida is generally warm, dry and sunny. Central and northern parts of the state can be a lot cooler, especially at night. Summers everywhere are hot and humid, with occasional thunderstorms. The odd hurricane can strike between June and November. Local newspapers and television give detailed forecasts, but note that Americans still measure temperatures in Fahrenheit.

Clothing
Take mainly lightweight clothing (cotton is most comfortable in summer), with an extra layer for cool evenings and icy air-conditioning. Dress in vacation areas is casual, although a few formal restaurants ask men to wear a jacket and tie. A raincoat, or at least an umbrella, may be useful at any time of year.

Communications
The telephone system, operated by a number of competing companies, is excellent. Dialling instructions are posted beside public telephones. To use them, have a supply of coins ready. For local calls, put one in the slot and dial

the seven digit number. The operator will tell you if an additional amount is needed.

For operator assistance, dial 0. For calls to a different area of the US, dial 1, plus the area code, then the seven digit number. Numbers beginning 1-800 are free. To make an international call, dial 011, then the country code (44 for UK), area code (omitting the initial zero) and number.

It generally costs much more to call from your hotel room, unless you use one of the calling cards issued by international telephone companies.

Fax messages can be sent and received through most hotels, which usually charge a fee per page, regardless of transmission time or destination.

Postal services are reasonably efficient but not rapid. Airmail reaches most European destinations in 4 to 6 days (2 days by the much more expensive express service). Stamps are sold at post offices and also (for more than face value) from machines in supermarkets, airports, etc. Post offices only deal with mail: to send a telegram, go to a Western Union office (or, with a credit card, use the telephone and dictate the message). It will be delivered the next day.

Parcel and courier services are widely used, within the US and internationally. They have pick-up points at some big hotels and supermarkets.

Crime

Big city crime rates are high, but with sensible precautions there is very little chance that you will be a victim. Strolling in city parks and side streets after dark is not recommended. Beware of pickpockets in crowded places, don't carry large amounts of cash, wear a minimum of jewellery and leave your valuables in your hotel safe. Be very careful about answering a knock on your hotel door; it's best to telephone the front desk for verification.

When driving, especially in the cities, plan your route to avoid unsafe areas—take local advice on where they are. Lock the car doors, keep windows closed (air-conditioning makes this bearable) and don't leave valuables on show, whether driving or parked. Particularly in Miami, be aware that fake "emergencies" may be staged to persuade drivers to stop: the police advise you *not* to do so. If you have a problem with your car, drive if possible to a well-lit service station before stopping.

Driving

Roads are mainly excellent, from the Interstate freeways (I numbers) which snake across the whole country to other national highways and state roads of various categories. On the few toll roads, known as turnpikes, charges are reasonable. Road numbering can help navigation: odd numbered roads go roughly north-south, evens east-west.

Drive on the right. You may turn right from the right lane, even when a traffic light is red (unless there's a "No Turn On Red" sign), provided you stop first, and give way to pedestrians and cross traffic.

Newcomers to the US will find lane discipline strange—there is no fast or slow lane except on some sections of interstate highway where signs tell slower traffic to keep right. So you may overtake or be overtaken on either side. Don't change lanes without a careful check, even though other drivers may weave alarmingly.

Speed limits are clearly signalled, in miles per hour. The maximum permitted on freeways in rural areas is 65 or 70 mph (105 or 112 kph). In residential areas it is typically 30–45 mph (48–72 kph). The degree of enforcement is unpredictable: some localities are very strict. Seatbelts must be worn. Don't drink and drive: "DWI" (driving while intoxicated) could result in your being locked up. When parked, the car must point in the same direction 59 as the traffic, or nose-in where parking is at an angle.

Petrol (gasoline or "gas"), and diesel fuel are widely available and cheap, at about a quarter of European prices (compensating for the greater distances and thirstier American cars). Normal unleaded fuel is adequate for most rental cars. It may be necessary to pay *before* filling, especially at night. Many pumps operate by inserting a credit card.

American motoring terms can differ from English usage: e.g. *yield* = give way; *traffic circle* = roundabout; *pass* = overtake; *detour* = diversion; *divided highway* = dual carriageway; *sidewalk* = pavement (and *pavement* = road). Parts of the car (automobile) have different names too: *parking brake* = handbrake; *trunk* = boot; *hood* = bonnet; *windshield* = windscreen.

Embassies and Consulates

Almost every nation on earth has an embassy in Washington DC, and some, mainly Latin American, countries also have consulates in Miami. Check the *Yellow Pages* directory in any city to find your country's nearest diplomatic representative.

Emergencies

To call the Police, Fire Department or for Medical Emergencies, telephone 911. The operator will ask which service you require.

Formalities

Currently, citizens of European Union countries and Switzerland holding a valid, individual machine-readable passport, with a return or onward ticket, do not need a visa for a stay of up to 90 days, *provided* they arrive by a regular air or sea carrier which participates in the visa waiver program (VWP). If you are travelling on an electronic ticket, you must carry a copy of your itinerary for presentation to US immigration at the port of entry. Check with your travel agent or the US embassy in your country well before leaving home. Visas for stays of more than 90 days are delivered by the US Embassy, after an interview by appointment only. Children must have their own passport. On arrival, all visitors between the ages of 14 and 79 are photographed and their fingerprints scanned.

On board, you will be given a US customs declaration form. Non-residents may take in gifts to a total value of $100, and a duty-free allowance of 200 cigarettes and 1 US quart (about 1 litre) of alcoholic drink. Anything more should be listed on the form. Personal property which you intend to take out of the country again need not be declared. Amounts over $10,000 in cash and/or travellers cheques must be declared. Fruit, vegetables and meats may not be imported—eat them or dispose of them before arrival, or in the bins provided before customs. Sniffer dogs are on duty to locate drugs, but food can interest them too.

Health

Any kind of medical treatment in the US is likely to be expensive, so be sure to arrange insurance to cover all eventualities.

After a long flight, relax for a couple of days. Doctors suggest eating lightly, and avoiding too much sun. In hot weather, drink plenty of water, wear a sunhat, use a sunscreen with a high protection factor (at least 20 and preferably more) and make sure that children do the same.

Languages

The English used in the USA may differ from that spoken in Britain, but films and TV have made it familiar. It's fun to spot new words and phrases. The rate of immigration means that other languages are often encountered; in Miami, you'll hear a lot of Spanish.

Media

Each US city has its own newspaper—sometimes more than one—but most of them focus on local news, although the *Miami Herald* has more international, especially Latin American, coverage. Friday, Saturday and Sunday editions are useful for finding out about entertainment and other events. Of the few papers distributed nationally, the best-known are *The New York Times*, with the most comprehensive international news, the *Wall Street Journal* covering business and finance, and *USA Today,* providing a lightweight summary.

National TV networks, local stations, satellite and cable channels are available in most hotels, sometimes with pay-per-view movie channels. CNN provides frequent news, round the clock.

Thousands of radio stations, mainly local, fill the wavebands with rock and pop, chat shows, phone-ins and hell-fire preachers. Somewhere in the cacophony you may find music to your taste, or something of interest on a Public Broadcasting Service (PBS) station.

Money

The US dollar ($) is divided into 100 cents (¢). Coins in wide use are the 1¢ (cent or penny), 5¢ (nickel), 10¢ (dime) and 25¢ (quarter). 50¢ coins are rarely used, and $1 coins are mainly confined to casinos. Banknotes (bills) in general circulation are $1, 5, 10, 20, 50 and 100, all the same size and colour; there are also $2 and $1000 bills but they are rare. Redesigned $10, $20 and $50 dollar bills have also been introduced, with different background colours and more security features.

Although foreign currency and travellers cheques may be changed at bigger banks or exchange offices, this can take time, so it is advisable to arrive with some cash and with travellers cheques in US dollars. Some hotels will change foreign money, but at an inferior rate.

All major credit cards are widely accepted in shops, hotels and restaurants (in some cases they are preferred to cash), but you may have to show extra identification. Cashpoints (ATMs: automatic teller machines) outside many banks will dispense money if you have the right card and know your PIN. Check with the issuing bank before your trip to confirm that the card will work in the US.

Opening Hours

Downtown shops generally open Monday to Saturday 10 a.m. to 6 p.m.; suburban shopping malls may keep longer hours and many open on Sunday.

Banks usually open Monday to Friday from 9 a.m. to 2 p.m., and some of them also open until noon on Saturday.

Most post offices open Monday to Friday from 8.30 a.m. to 5 p.m., and some main branches open Saturday morning.

Photography and Video

All kinds of film and videotape are available. Colour prints can be quickly and cheaply processed, but transparency film is probably best taken back to your own country for developing. Note that pre-recorded video tapes are incompatible with European systems (unless specially made for export).

Public Holidays

January 1	*New Year's Day*
Third Mon. in January	*Martin Luther King Day*
Third Mon. in February	*Presidents' Day*
Last Mon. in May	*Memorial Day*
July 4	*Independence Day*
First Mon. in September	*Labor Day*
Second Mon. in October	*Columbus Day*
November 11	*Veterans' Day*
Fourth Thurs. in November	*Thanksgiving*
December 25	*Christmas*
Moveable holiday:	*Easter Monday*

Public Transport

Airlines and long-distance buses, most operated by Greyhound, connect the main cities, and in a few cases trains are a viable alternative. In general, however, a rental car is the best way to get around. Within the cities there are buses, and Miami has a commuter rail system. Metered taxis are readily available.

Religion

More than one American in two is a regular church-goer. The numerous Protestant faiths include Baptist, Methodist and Presbyterian. Catholics are fewer in number, but nevertheless total more than 50 million. The Jewish community is particularly influential, and recent immigration has led to the growth of the Muslim, Hindu and Buddhist communities.

Churches, synagogues, temples and mosques are listed in the *Yellow Pages,* and weekend editions of local newspapers give the times of services.

Time

Florida is on Eastern Standard Time (GMT –5), advancing one hour to Eastern Daylight Time (GMT –4) from April to October. Thus for most of the year it is six hours behind mainland Europe and five hours behind the UK and Ireland.

Tipping

In restaurants, a tip of around 15% is expected—and Americans often give even more for exceptional service. Bar staff expect to be tipped. Gratuities are rarely included on the bill and they make up a significant part of the staff's income. Taxi drivers and tour guides are tipped about 10-15%.

Toilets

More often known by euphemisms such as restroom or bathroom, these are found in hotels, restaurants, department stores, supermarkets and petrol (gas) stations. They're generally clean and efficient.

Tourist Information

Cities and many smaller towns have tourist offices which can provide excellent brochures, maps and other information. Airports and city centres may have information desks, and you can find the address of the local Convention and Visitors Bureau in telephone directories. Staff are usually enthusiastic and helpful.

Voltage

The electrical supply is 110V, 60 cycles AC (60 Hz). Plugs have two flat parallel pins; a few have an additional round pin. Most European equipment needs a transformer as well as an adaptor.

INDEX

BAHAMAS

Sun, Sand and Sea

Strewn over a vast expanse of the Atlantic Ocean, the Bahamas bask in breezy, semi-tropical sunshine. Out of about 700 islands, around 100 are at least minimally inhabited, though only a few dozen have vacation facilities. Another 2,400 smaller cays (pronounced "keys") are blissfully deserted. Nassau, on New Providence Island, the capital city of the Commonwealth of the Bahamas, and Freeport on Grand Bahama Island are the main population centres.

Starting as close as 80 km (50 miles) to the Florida coast, the archipelago swoops southeast for 1000 km (600 miles) almost to Haiti and eastern Cuba. This strategic location along the major shipping routes between the Caribbean and North America has been a crucial factor in the history of the islands. Ever since Christopher Columbus came ashore on the Bahamian island of San Salvador in 1492 (the actual landfall is contested), wreckers, pirates, rum runners and modern smugglers have been among those who found the thousands of reefs, cays and coves useful.

The great glory of these islands is the incredible sea lapping their shores. The water is so clear you hardly need a snorkel mask to

enjoy the astonishing array of marine life at countless coral reefs. Some of the dive scenes in the James Bond blockbusters were filmed in these waters. Divers can explore fish-filled holes and seek the wrecks of the many treasure ships which came to grief over centuries in the treacherous shoals of what the Spaniards called *baja mar* (shallow sea). From that came the anglicized name, Bahamas.

Tourism is overwhelmingly the nation's biggest business. Nassau, Paradise Island and Freeport have been specifically designed for holiday pleasure and are jam-packed much of the time with visitors determinedly pursuing it. Yachts glide gingerly into cluttered marinas; barefoot children cruise resort beaches hawking shell necklaces to row upon row of glistening sunbathers; camera-clicking holiday-makers bob and sway in overworked glass-bottom boats; honeymooners hold hands (and their breath) as the casino roulette wheels spin on and on.

And while there's plenty of goodwill about being helpful to tourists, there is rarely any great hurry about getting things done. "We have three speeds," you may hear a Bahamian explain, "slow, stop and reverse".

BAHAMAS

A Brief History

15th–16th centuries	Christopher Columbus lands in the Bahamas (perhaps Watling Island, now called San Salvador, or Samana Cay, or Egg Island off Eleuthera) on October 12, 1492. Disappointed in his search for gold and other riches, he sails out of the Bahamas towards neighbouring Cuba. The Spanish remove the Indian inhabitants of Lucaya on Grand Bahama Island to work in Spain, Haiti and Cuba.
17th century	A group of English Puritans from Bermuda establish the first permanent European settlement on Eleuthera in 1648, followed in 1666 by a second colony on New Providence Island. Charles II of England grants the Bahamas to six Lords Proprietors, who are powerless to suppress the piracy that rages in the archipelago. The Spanish attack Nassau, but the pirates are undeterred. Blackbeard, Henry Morgan and other corsairs operate out of Nassau.
18th century	The Bahamas become a crown colony in 1718. The first royal governor cleans out the pirates and calls an Assembly. Spain rules the islands for one year in 1782, but the Treaty of Versailles (1783) returns them to the British. Cotton plantations flourish but prosperity is short-lived. The weak soil is soon depleted and a plague destroys crops. Most planters leave. Nassau becomes a free port in 1787.
19th century	Slavery, never widespread, is officially abolished in the 1830s. The Confederate States are supplied from the Bahamas during the American Civil War. The sponge industry (later destroyed by fungus) is introduced.
20th century–present	During the first two decades massive emigration takes place, mainly to the United States. During Prohibition, Nassau booms as a centre for bootlegging. The city's first gambling casino opens in 1920, and an air service links Nassau to Miami nine years later. An offshore banking boom begins in the 1930s. During World War II American bases are established in the Bahamas and the Duke of Windsor becomes governor. Tourism increases steadily, especially after the Cuban revolution. The Bahamas achieve self-government and, in 1973, independence. In the 1980s the country's place at the centre of international finance declines: there are rumours of money laundering and new Caribbean banking competition to contend with.

New Providence Island

With its hotel glitter and restaurant sophistication, its daytime traffic jams and night-time naughtiness, **Nassau** (population 205,000) is certainly not typical of the Bahamas. But it's definitely a magnet for tourists. **Bay Street** is the commercial centre of the city, but the traditional tourist hub is the **Straw Market** at Market Plaza. The amiable sales ladies here have been creating straw items since childhood.

The picture-postcard **Public Buildings** dating from 1812 and a bleached marble statue of a young, seated Queen Victoria recall the British colonial era.

The town's oldest and most interesting building is the **Public Library** of 1797, between Shirley Street and the Court House. The seashell collection in the entry has some rarities, but the really interesting things are upstairs: fine old prints, maps and portraits, a carved stone Arawak ceremonial stool and other artefacts.

A white statue of a dashing Columbus commands steep steps up to pink **Government House** (closed to the public), residence of governors and governor-generals for nearly two centuries.

Christ Church Cathedral (Anglican) in George Street, a

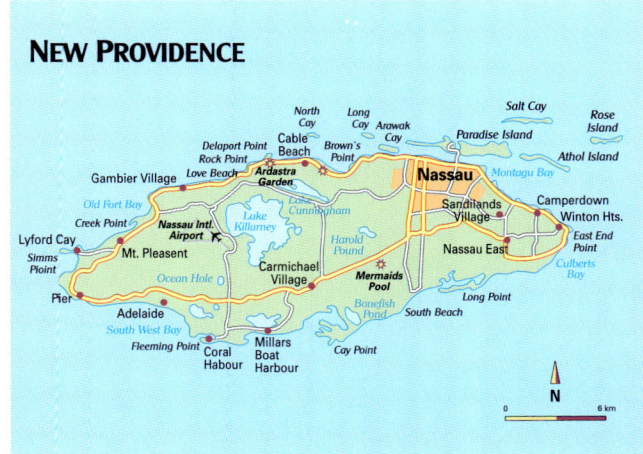

pleasantly airy building with a dark timbered roof, was constructed in 1841, while the three-storey **Deanery** in Cumberland Street dates from about 1710 and may be the oldest residence in the Bahamas.

Slaves hacked the **Queen's Staircase** in Elizabeth Avenue from the black rock cliff as a passageway for troops garrisoned above at Fort Fincastle. At the top, you'll reach Nassau's water tower which offers a stunning **panorama** of New Providence and the harbour.

West of Nassau there's no missing the grey stone ramparts of **Fort Charlotte**, named after the consort of George III. Tourists are escorted into the dungeon which houses a mock-up of a torture chamber complete with stretching rack, though it never held prisoners. Beneath Fort Charlotte, the **Nassau Botanical Gardens** display a variety of carefully kept tropical flowers and plants. In the same area, the flowers take back seat to the remarkable attraction of marching flamingoes at **Ardastra Gardens**. Elsewhere around this mini-zoo, look for peacocks, a croc and an iguana.

At **Coral World** marine observatory, you'll see a sample of the incredible underwater life of

the Bahamas. It's said to be the biggest man-made coral reef in the world.

Further west is the **Cable Beach** resort area, where excitement and amusements abound.

One of the best beaches is past Northwest Point at **Old Fort Bay**. This gentle arc of soft sand is backed by dense foliage in which stand the remains of an old fort.

Small, isolated and charmingly unspoiled, **Adelaide Village** on Southwest Bay dates back to 1832 when it was settled by slaves freed from ships stopped by the Royal Navy. A prominent sign announces the next "Be Healed Revival Meeting".

Back in Nassau look for **Blackbeard's Tower**, said to be a lookout built by the 17th-century pirate chief, strategically perched on a hillock overlooking the eastern approach to Nassau harbour. The tower is along a short path off Eastern Road, meandering back to town past scores of lovely homes. From this end of town, a toll bridge crosses over to Paradise Island, and beneath the bridge is some of the best fun Nassau has to offer: **Potters Cay**, where all day long little fishing boats tie up with conch, turtle, grouper and snapper, which are soon snapped up by householders and restaurateurs.

Paradise Island

"Welcome to Paradise" says the sign just after you've paid your bridge toll. Pearly gates there aren't, yet, but you immediately see tall casuarina trees and palms, which cover much of this renowned resort island. If you choose, take a ferry instead from Rawson Square, or make the 5-minute crossing on foot.

For centuries the sliver of an islet was uninhabited, but it has now been developed into a complete "destination within a destination". It boasts hotels, casino and cabarets, extensive facilities for golf and other sports, a marina called Hurricane Hole, and the Atlantis waterpark with a lagoon that's home to sharks, barracudas and sting rays. Of the excellent beaches strung out along the island's north shore, **Paradise Beach** is the best known.

Toward the eastern end of the island are the **Versailles Gardens** with statuary adorning a long row of manicured terraces and its **French Cloister**. Originally built in the 14th century by Augustinian monks in Montréjeau near Lourdes, France, the cloister was shipped here in pieces for reconstruction 600 years later.

The biggest bargain on Paradise Island is watching the **dolphins** being fed each afternoon in the mid-island lagoon near the Britannia Towers.

The waters around **Athol Island**, east of Paradise Island, are filled with wrecks, coral colonies and tropical fish, easily viewed by glass-bottom boat.

Grand Bahama Island

The commercial and resort centre of **Freeport/Lucaya** is even less typical of the Bahamas than Nassau. Despite English place names and tours by red London double-decker bus, basic Bahamian local colour is in short supply here. The atmosphere is more palpably American than anywhere else in the Commonwealth—not unexpectedly, since it was a Virginia financier, Wallace Groves, who conceived the "Freeport miracle" and set it in motion in 1955. (Under the Hawksbill Creek agreement of that year, a deep-water harbour was decided upon along with the tax and duty-free port. Tourism began to boom when the first casino opened in 1964.) Most of the island's 47,000 residents live in this city—or at the West End settlement 40 km (25 miles) away. Landscaped highways, clearly signposted and even at times divided, connect modern hotels with marinas, golf courses, and shopping and gambling complexes.

The **International Bazaar**, an unusual mixture of architecture and offerings from various parts of the world, is Freeport's major

The glory of the Bahamas is its clear blue sea.

sightseeing attraction, and worth wandering through even if you're not planning on buying from any of the scores of shops. Built in 1967, it was the work of a Hollywood set designer. The restored 18th-century Bahamian mansion next door houses a perfume factory, where essences from the world over are blended and bottled. Close by is the huge **El Casino**, with its strange Moorish façade, near the island's main straw market, where ladies with broad smiles are used to posing for photographs. Major hotels 73 and golf courses are also in the area. The atmosphere is more authentically Bahamian at the native fruit and vegetable market, an all-weather cluster of family stalls in Churchill Square, and at the occasional fairs, parades and "jumpin'" religious events.

East of Freeport's central attractions, the sprawling **Lucaya** resort area features beachfront and marina hotels, the island's best golf courses and several sightseeing possibilities. A fierce competitor to Freeport's International Bazaar is the huge **Port Lucaya** complex, combining shops and entertainment.

"Please do not touch the plants—many are poisonous", says the sign at the **Garden of the Groves**. That's the only jarring note in these thoroughly delightful 4.5 ha (11 acres) of tropical flora, man-made waterfalls and ponds. Lizards dart by as you stroll among the 10,000 plants and trees. The **Grand Bahama Museum**, within the garden, is worth visiting for its exhibitions on the history of the Lucayan Indians, the Bahamas' earliest settlers, undersea life and costumes from the Junkanoo, a Bahamian festival that has its origins in Africa.

From Bell Channel Bay, wind conditions permitting, what's billed as the world's largest **glass-bottom boat** takes tourists over

coral gardens and along Grand Bahama's deep reef. Sharks, barracudas, stingrays and other intriguing creatures can usually be spotted.

Undersea buffs might enjoy the **Museum of Underwater Exploration** at the Underwater Explorers Society in the same inlet. Apart from various items brought up by divers, some early underwater gear is on display, including primitive-looking cameras and masks. Around the diving facilities in the area, by the way, you're bound to hear about the million or more dollars worth of Spanish pieces-of-eight found offshore from Lucaya in 1964. The shallow site, long since stripped of its gold, is nicknamed Treasure Reef. The diving school of the Underwater Explorers Society offers a unique amusement called the **"Dolphin Experience"**, in which you can swim and dive with these intelligent, friendly mammals. If your time is not limited, visit the **Lucaya National Park**, with both natural forest and mangrove swamp.

To the north, on East-Settlers Way, the **Rand Memorial Nature Centre** offers 90-minute guided walks with a naturalist through a protected Bahamian forest, a chance to photograph flamingoes and other uncommon birds and to spot 21 different kinds of wild orchids.

To the west of Freeport is the settlement of **Eight Mile Rock**. Mysteriously, a number of old cannonballs have been found in this area in recent times, though not even pirates are supposed to have lived on Grand Bahama until the 1840s.

Signs make good reading along the road, as you pass such places as **Sea Grape, Deadman's Reef** and **Bottle Bay**. Near Holmes Rock, **Hydro Flora Gardens,** a small nursery, offers a tour and lecture on tropical plants grown without soil.

West End, sadly, isn't the roguish place it used to be. Searching the sleepy seaside village, you'll find only the scantiest traces of the bad old days of prohibition when merchants and rum runners made fortunes smuggling liquor into the "dry" United States. A few old-timers recall the bootlegging boom days when a boat owned by Al Capone was loaded with booze here.

In the "gin clear" water just offshore in front of the aged Star Hotel landmark and the so-called Old Factory, you'll see some concrete slabs of Prohibition-era piers and bits of old iron rails used to roll contraband down to waiting boats. In this oldest Grand Bahama settlement there are six churches and a multitude of bars or clubs, mostly small wooden affairs. West End's few inhabitants don't benefit as much as they'd like from the large, self-sustaining tourist hotel complex which dominates the area. From here you can go on deep-sea fishing and scuba-diving excursions.

Tourists won't normally find it convenient to take the bus which goes most days between Freeport and the eastern end of the island. By taxi or rented car, it's a long drive on a road which deteriorates dramatically once past the US Air Force missile tracking installations around **High Rock**. From the road you'll see impressive radar dishes and antennae, but stern signs prohibit closer inspection. On this trip you parallel the majority of Grand Bahama's advertised 60 miles (100 km) of beaches, most of them long, windswept stretches frequented only by birds and crabs. Tiny **Pelican Point** is a tidy, friendly roadside settlement where the centre of all things is the Baptist church.

McLean's Town, metropolis of the east end, has a few hundred inhabitants who live in pastel wooden houses. The settlement is unusual in that the majority of the women go out fishing for a living, as do the menfolk. They bring in snapper, grouper, conch, porgy and crawfish. A bit shy at first, villagers are genuinely pleased to welcome strangers. They'll be happy to tell you about the town's biggest event of the year, the Conch Cracking Contest held on Discovery Day, October 12, when great crowds turn up to watch competitors crack, empty and clean up to 25 conches in less than three minutes.

At a fishing camp on nearby **Deep Water Cay**, you'll hear other sea sagas from the regulars. There's very good bone-fishing in the shallows among the east end mangroves, and collecting seashells (shelling) can be superb along such beaches as **Crabbin Bay** and **John Davis**.

Out Islands

The islands and cays "out and away" from the hubs of Nassau and Freeport are called collectively the Out Islands (or sometimes the Family Islands). These are some of the most popular ones.

The Abacos

Many of the cays in this archipelago north of New Providence were founded by Loyalists from New England and the Carolinas at the time of the American Revolution, and a number of the towns still have something of a New England air about them—it's been called Cape Cod with palm trees.

A 200-year-old tradition of shipbuilding is still in evidence in **Man-O-War Cay**. The town is the home of the famous Abaco dinghy, the sturdy sailboat that was the work boat of the Bahamian fishermen and traders for two centuries. You're invited to watch as carpenters meticulously handcraft each boat. These days, many are built of fibreglass, but the craftsmanship is the same as in the days of wood and canvas.

Green Turtle Cay is the site of one of the oldest settlements on the outer cays. The village of **New Plymouth** was founded by loyalists in 1783. It was once the second-largest settlement in the Bahamas after Nassau. Today about 500 people live here, and they are some of the friendliest people you'll ever meet. New Plymouth still looks much like it did in the 18th century, a small New England fishing village. Flower-bordered lanes lead past clapboard houses charmingly decorated in Victorian gingerbread. Some of the landmarks are the old colonial jail, where you can have your picture taken "behind bars", a 200-year-old cemetery, the 150-year-old Commissioner's Office and the Albert Lowe Memorial Museum, with an outstanding collection of colonial artefacts. A must-see is a local tavern, "Miss Emily's Blue Bee Bar", where you can sample the famous Goombay Smash made with local rum and fruit juice.

The Abaco archipelago has some of the best diving and snorkelling sites in the Bahamas, notably in **Pelican Cay National Park**, with possibilities for night dives. **Marsh Harbour** on Great Abaco island is the bare-boat charter centre of the northern Bahamas. At nearby Hope Town, if you're feeling energetic, climb the 100 steps of the pink-and-white candy-striped lighthouse for a picturesque view.

Treasure Cay boasts more good leisure facilities, with an 18-hole championship golf course and tennis courts.

Eleuthera

Outstanding tourist amenities abound in this "garden island" rich in verdant farms and pineapple plantations, and endowed with beautiful beaches and fantastic dive sites.

Off the northern coast, accessible by water ferry, is the "prettiest island", **Harbour Island**, famous for its sheltered pink beach and the beautiful village of Dunmore Town. The original capital of the Bahamas, it is a photographer's dream with its clapboard houses and gardens of hibiscus, bougainvillaea and oleander.

Cat Island

Wide beaches, deep creeks, pre-Columbian Arawak Indian caves, and fertile, scenic hills are the attractions here. On the highest "peak", 60 m (206 ft) high, stands the monastery of Mount Alvernia, once home of the hermit-monk Father Jerome.

San Salvador

The site long thought to be Columbus's first landing in the New World is another favourite of scuba divers and game fishing.

Long Island

Columbus claimed that this green and fertile island was the most beautiful he had ever seen. Sharing the coastline with rugged cliffs are scores of dazzling white sand beaches. More than 30 shipwrecks can be explored off nearby Conception Island.

Exumas

Yachtsmen love to cruise this long string of mostly uninhabited isles and cays. Nobody has managed to count all of the pristine beaches and coves. Several large resorts are clustered around Elizabeth Harbour on Great Exuma. Inland are some poignant ruins of once-great plantation houses.

Andros

This island claims the world's third-largest reef, a scuba and snorkel wonderland. Beyond the reef, the ocean bottom descends rapidly to a depth of 8 km (5 miles)—called the "Tongue of the Ocean"—where the fishing is fabulous. The interior of Andros is still basically untouched.

Bimini

Anglers also congregate here, the self-styled fishing capital of the world. Writer Ernest Hemingway brought the island fame when he lived in Blue Marlin Cottage in Alice Town. The local museum has mementos of his stay.

Berry Islands

The 30 cays in the archipelago amount to a total of only about 30 sq km (11 sq miles), but there are some chic resort facilities and superb sport fishing in the nearby "Tongue of the Ocean". Boaters find much to revel in here, as do golfers (at Great Harbour Cay) and beach connoisseurs.

Crooked Island

Quaint villages clustering along the creeks and tidal flats, magnificent beaches where yours may be the only footprints on the sand, a bone-fishing paradise—yet this southern island is one of the least explored.

Great Inagua

The southernmost island of the archipelago is one of the biggest, but one of the least visited. It is known for two things: an important production of salt, and Lake Windsor, part of the Bahamas National Park, where thousands of flamingos come to mate each spring. Tours can be arranged through the Bahamas National Trust in Nassau.

Dining Out

Local chefs specialize in some interesting seafood variations, many of which contain conch. This chewy mollusc is prepared in a multitude of ways: fried, stewed, in soup (conch chowder), in salad (with onions, celery, sweet and hot peppers and tomatoes). Grouper, a flaky white fish, is the most popular in the Bahamas, but don't pass by red snapper in anchovy sauce either. Crab and spiny lobster come steamed, creamed, minced, grilled, baked, stewed, devilled or stuffed. Peas'n'rice, a traditional accompaniment, is a national passion.

For dessert try guava duff—a pie made from the local aromatic guava fruit, served with rum sauce—or simply some fresh fruit from the islands.

Rum figures in a whole gamut of tropical drinks. Have it in *piña colada* (with coconut cream and pineapple juice), Yellow Bird (with coffee, banana liqueur and fruit juices) or Skinny Minnie (with Galliano, cream, Cointreau

coconut liqueur and grenadine), to name but a few. The local liqueur is Nassau Royal, good by itself or in coffee. Leading American soft drinks are sold everywhere, but for a refreshing change try canned sea grape soda.

Shopping

Local craftsmen who have resisted mass-production to satisfy surging tourist demand produce some distinctive souvenirs. Coconut-shell artefacts and jewellery are said to be nearly indestructible. Conch shell, whelk shell or sharks' teeth may also be used. Printed fabrics, particularly batiks from Andros, are hand-waxed and dyed with colourful island designs. Straw goods take in everything from sunhats and carry-alls to straw aeroplanes complete with pilot or straw models of Nassau surreys. Wood-carvings are also popular.

Rum is a firm favourite, especially Eleuthera pineapple rum and the coconut variety.

Freeport/Lucaya's bonded area offers a range of tax-exempt European and Commonwealth goods at attractive prices: china, cutlery, fabrics, glass, leather, perfumes, silver, watches, cameras and spirits. Nassau is advertised as one of the best places to buy duty-free watches; also look for jewellery, crystal, china, leather and spirits here.

Practical Information

Banks
Open Monday to Thursday 9.30 a.m. to 3 p.m., Friday to 5 p.m.

Clothing
Pack casual, lightweight resort wear. People tend to dress up at night. A jacket or sweater can come in handy both for arctic air-conditioning and cool evening breezes. It is frowned on to wear beach attire in towns.

Currency
The Bahamian dollar is pegged to American currency and divided into 100 cents. Coins range from 1 to 25 cents; banknotes from 50 cents to $100. US dollars are also accepted. Major credit cards are widely accepted in the larger establishments.

Restaurants
Lunch is served from noon to 2.30 p.m.; dinner from 7 p.m. to 10 p.m. or later.

Shops
Open daily 9 a.m. to 5 p.m., except Sundays, and also one afternoon a week (Thursday, Friday or Saturday).

Telephone
Nassau (area code 242) is linked to the US network.To call the UK, dial 011 44, then the area code and local number.

Time
GMT–5, with summer time GMT–4.

Tipping
Many hotels and restaurants automatically include a service charge on the bill, but where this is not the case 15 per cent is customary for most services, including taxis.

GENERAL EDITOR
Barbara Ender

PHOTO CREDITS
CORBIS/Darrell Gulin: p. 1
CORBIS/Joseph Sohm, p. 8
CORBIS/Alan Schein, p. 13
Claude Hervé-Bazin:
pp. 2, 20, 24, 27, 30, 35, 46
Frances/hemis.fr: pp. 5, 11, 73
Busson/hemis.fr: p. 65
Martine Gaillard: p. 16
Bernard Joliat: pp. 32, 40, 53
Philip H. Coblentz: p. 77

MAPS
Elsner & Schichor;
Huber Kartographie;
JPM Publications

Copyright © 2006, 1997
JPM Publications S.A.
12, avenue William-Fraisse,
1006 Lausanne, Suisse
information@jpmguides.com
http://www.jpmguides.com/

Printed in Switzerland – 06/06/01
Weber/Bienne
Edition 2006–2007

FLORIDA

N

0   50 km

Atlantic Ocean

Gulf of Mexico

GEORGIA

Okefenokee Swamp

Thomasville
Quitman
Valdosta
Homerville
Monticello
Greenville
Jasper
Live Oak
Perry
Mayo
Capps
Falmouth
Taylor
Callahan
Yulee
Fernandina Beach
Amelia Island
Baldwin
Sanderson
Jacksonville
Hampton Springs
Salem
Lake City
Branford
High Sprs.
Lake Butler
Middleburg
Green Cove Springs
Jacksonville Beach
Dekle Beach
Steinhatchee
Old Town
Gainesville
Alachua
Waldo
Starke
Keystone Hts.
Boswick
Palatka
Spuds
St. Augustine
St. Johns River
Chiefland
Archer
Hawthorne
San Mateo
Fowler Bluff
Williston
Citra
Salt Springs
Lake George
Bunnell
Palm Coast
Cedar Key
Cedar Key
Sumner
Otter Creek
Ocala
Lynne
Barberville
De Leon Springs
Ormond Beach
Yankeetown
Dunnellon
Belleview
Daytona Beach
Waccasassa Bay
Crystal River
Hernando
Lady Lake
De Land
Deltona
New Smyrna Beach
Homosassa Islands
Homosassa
Leesburg
Eustis
Tavares
Sanford
Oak Hill
Inverness
Clermont
Orlando
Titusville
Brooksville
Rich Manor
John F. Kennedy Space Center
Spring Hill
Disney World
Port St. John
Bayonet Point
Dade City
Zephyrhills
Sea World
Kissimmee
Cape Canaveral
Merrit Island
Tarpon Springs
Land O'Lakes
St. Cloud
Holopaw
Melbourne
Clearwater
Plant City
Lakeland
Haines City
Palm Bay
Tampa
Mulberry
Bartow
Winter Haven
Lake Kissimmee
Orchid Island
St. Petersburg
Tampa Bay
Lake Wales
Kenansville
Sebastian
Duette
Torrey
Avon Park
Jeehaw Junction
Vero Beach
Bradenton
Parrish
Sebring
Fort Drum
Fort Pierce
Bradenton Beach
Verna
Zolfo Springs
Hutchinson Island
Longboat Key
Lake Placid
Okeechobee
Stuart
Sarasota
Arcadia
St. Lucie Inlet
Hobe Sound
Fort Ogden
Palmdale
Venice
Jupiter
Lake Okeechobee
North Port
Port Charlotte
Riviera Beach
Gasparilla Island
Punta Gorda
Pahokee
West Palm Beach
Charlotte Harbor
Cape Coral
Fort Myers
Clewiston
Belle Glade
Lake Worth
Boca Grande
Lehigh Acres
Boynton Beach
Captiva
Immokalee
Seminole Indian Reservation
Delray Beach
Sanibel Island
Boca Raton
Deerfield Beach
Pompano Beach
Weston
Fort Lauderdale
Naples
The Everglades
Hollywood
North Miami Beach
Marco Island
Tamiami Trail
Hialeah
Miami Beach
Miami
Everglades City
Miccosukee
Key Biscayne
Kendall
Coral Gables
Homestead
Biscayne National Park
Florida City
Everglades National Park
Mangrove Swamp
John Pennekamp State Park
Flamingo
Florida Bay
Key Largo
Islamorada
Layton
Long Key
Bahia Honda State Park
Grassy Key
Marathon
Duck Key
Pine Islands
Summerland Key
Seven Mile Bridge
Florida Keys
Key West

USA
Florida
Bahamas
Mexico
Cuba
Dominican Republic
Belize
Haiti
Puerto Rico
Guatemala
Honduras
El Salvador
Nicaragua
Costa Rica
Panama
Venezuela
Guyana
Colombia
Brazil

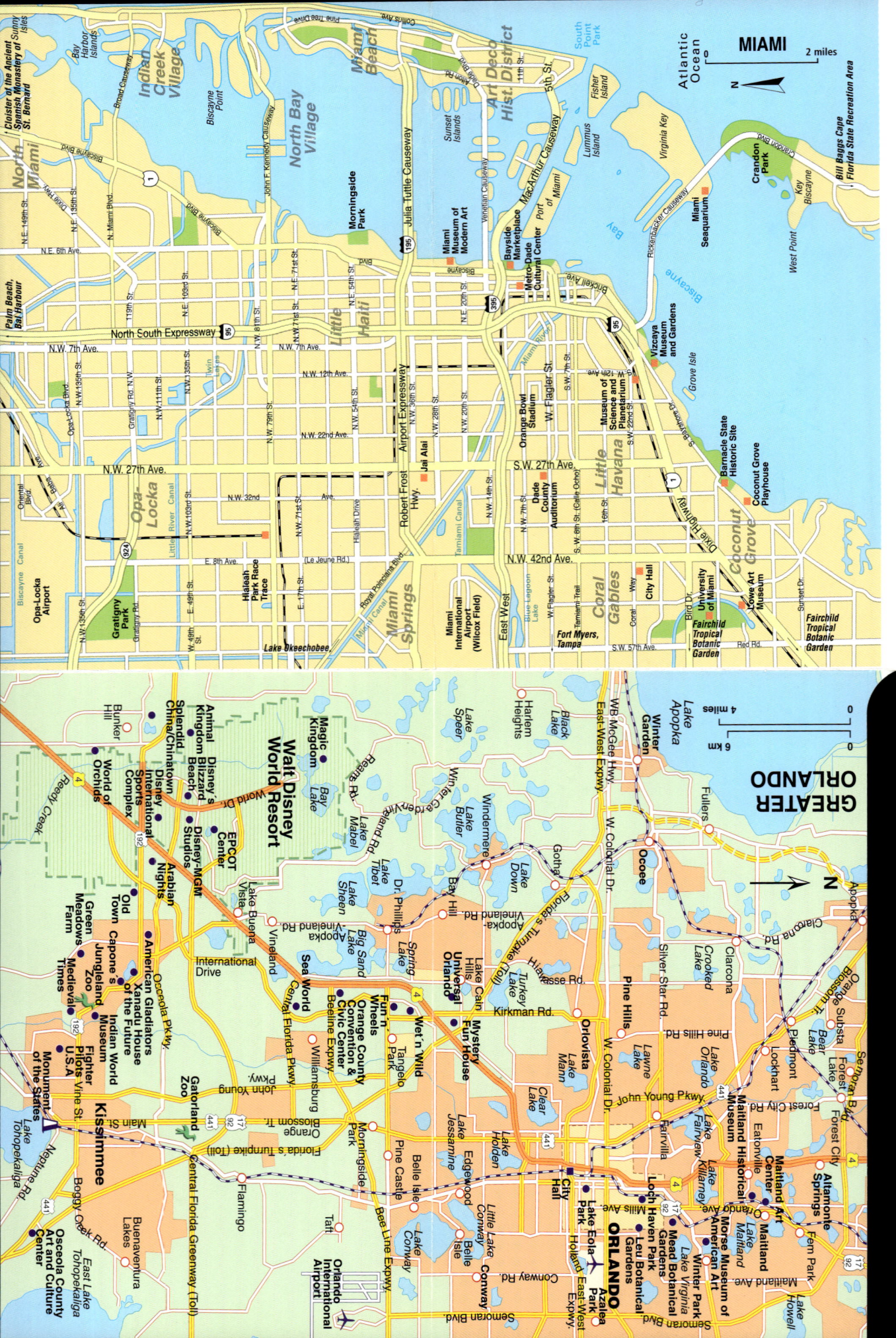